The Book of
Wellspring

by
Richard and Phyllis Beauvais

Copyright © 2020 by Richard and Phyllis Beauvais

ISBN: 978-1688917309

All rights reserved. No portion of this book may be copied, retransmitted, reposted, duplicated, or otherwise used without the express written approval of the author, except by reviewers who may quote excerpts in connection with a review.

CONTENTS

Preface 7

Introduction 9

Chapter 1: The Foundation – Wellspring's Mission, Philosophy, and Values 13

    The Discovery 14

    Mission Statement, Treatment Philosophy, and Core Values 14

        Personal 15

        Relational 15

    Treatment as Intensive 17

    Treatment as Comprehensive 18

    The Wellspring Logo – A Symbol of Wellspring's Values 19

Chapter 2: The History of Wellspring 21

    Origins of Wellspring's Philosophy and Values 22

        Daytop 24

        The Philosophy (No Refuge) – Poem Authored by Richard Beauvais 26

        The Country Place 27

        Jungian Psychology 29

        The Abbey of Regina Laudis 31

    A Brief Chronological History 34

        1977 to 1994 34

        1994 to 1999 36

        1999 to 2002 38

        2002 to 2007 39

        2007 to 2011 40

        2011 to 2019 42

    The Path Forward 44

Chapter 3: Wellspring's Person-Centered, Relational Approach 47

    Recovering the Person in Treatment 48

The Therapeutic Use of Personality 50
Therapeutic Parenting 53
Therapeutic Community as a Healing Theater for the Self 57
The Importance of Safe, Healing Touch in Treatment 58
Conclusion 58

Chapter 4: Intensive and Comprehensive: Wellspring's Model of Residential Treatment 61
Intensive Residential Treatment Supports Transition 62
An Integrated Model of Care 65

Chapter 5: Wellspring's Residential and School Programs 71
Adolescent Girls Residential Treatment Program-Beauvais House 73
Girls Residential Treatment Program-Shiloah House 75
Adult Women's Residential Treatment Program-Angelus House 76
Arch Bridge School 78

Chapter 6: Collaborative Convergence: Therapeutic Modes in Wellspring's
Integrated Holistic Approach 83
The Clinical "Backbone": Individual and Family Therapy and the
Medical Dimension of Care 85
Expressive Therapy 85
Work Program 86
Animal Program 90
Garden Programs 93
Adventure Program 96
Art Therapy 96
Sandtray Therapy 97
Conclusion 99

Chapter 7: Centering in the Still Point 101

Credits and Acknowledgements 105

PREFACE

Fifty years ago, on July 3, 1967, I met Richard Beauvais walking down Dogwood Road in Bolinas, California. He had come to seek me out at the encouragement of a mutual friend, because we were both poets. We spent three intensive days together working on his poetry. And dancing. He then returned to Connecticut and we had no contact for three years. Each of us, separately, was engaged in our own work of formation. On July 3, 1970, we reconnected; after three months, we were married. We worked together at The Country Place in Litchfield for seven years, and then we founded Wellspring. Now, over forty years later, we offer this book as a partial record.

Wellspring is, to us, an ever-unfolding miracle. Through incomprehensible grace, we have been privileged to serve its Spirit-driven mission, imperfect as we are. The work is good. It is hard. It is meaningful.

Richard died in January 2019, at the age of 80 – just over 41 years after Wellspring's founding. Hundreds of people – many of them associated with Wellspring – gathered to mourn his passing and celebrate his life. Many of them wrote or spoke – testifying to Richard's work and mission as a healer, to the lives he saved and those he helped shape.

This is Richard's book. He is, among other things, a historian. He labored over these past few years to set down what he could, to provide a way for others to discover and embrace this mission. We who are left behind have now finished what he started – rearranging and stitching together the pieces into a whole, like one of my great grandmother's Nebraska quilts.

In some ways, the book is not complete. So many people have not been named – board, staff, residents, students, families, donors, friends – each person who has been called to contribute to the work of Wellspring is a part of the indelible story of this remarkably blessed place.

You know who you are.

You are written forever into the deeper Book of Wellspring.

Phyllis Beauvais

Wellspring co-founder

INTRODUCTION

I am honored to introduce *The Book of Wellspring*, which encompasses a series of original essays and articles by Richard and Phyllis Beauvais, our co-founders – together with material based on writings by Wellspring staff and Richard's interviews with staff. This collection helps tell the story of Wellspring, a psychotherapeutic and educational center that has grown organically from its small beginnings in 1977, serving thousands of children, adolescents, adults and families with emotional, relational and mental health challenges.

It will introduce you to these two amazing people who took an incredible leap of faith in creating this remarkable center. Wellspring is a source of healing that flows from their seminal ideas and values, which are reflected in Wellspring's Mission Statement:

> *Wellspring is a therapeutic and educational center dedicated to healing and learning through relational approaches – to self, others, creation and Spirit – which touch and bring forth the wellspring of personal being unique to each individual, giving hope to each person and family in our care.*

The core treatment values at the heart of our mission follow from that statement: *Therefore, our programs and services:*

- *Are designed in a comprehensive and holistic way to be responsive to the mind, heart, body and spirit of each person;*

- *Are intensive, so as to provide the personal intimacy, safety and professional capacity to address – in depth – the relevant treatment and educational objectives;*

- *Support the integrity of the family, its healthy reconstitution, and the personal growth of each individual involved;*

- *Provide a safe, healthy environment for residents, students, clients, and staff;*

- *Communicate a reverence for social diversity, biodiversity, and nature's beauty in a way that encourages the extension of personal relationship to all of creation.*

Underscoring Wellspring's mission and values is a statement of faith held to throughout our history:

> *Our guiding belief is that through the integrity and spirit with which we live and mediate these core values with each of the persons we serve, the Spirit will continue to support and guide us in our endeavors.*

This book is based on a collection of works written piecemeal over the 40-plus years of this foundation. Richard, Phyllis, and others have stitched these works together – as Phyllis writes in the Preface – into a quilt. Many of the pieces – chapters and sections of chapters – stand on their own and can be appreciated as such. Nevertheless, this quilt has a design and can be appreciated as a whole. It begins, in Chapter 1, with an introduction to Wellspring's mission and core values. Chapter 2 provides a brief history of Wellspring – an account of the ideas and experiences in which this foundation is rooted, as well as a chronology of its growth and development over the last forty-plus years. The following two chapters take a deeper cut at Wellspring's model of treatment – including the values of *personal* and *relational* care (Chapter 3) and our *intensive* and *comprehensive* approach to residential treatment (Chapter 4). Chapter 5 – drawn from Richard's interviews of and writing by staff – provides an account of Wellspring's major residential and school programs as they exist today, with particular attention to the culture of each therapeutic "milieu." Chapter 6 – again drawn from staff writings and interviews – turns to a more in-depth account of the various therapeutic modalities at Wellspring, including Emotional Expressive Therapy, our land-based programs (Animal Program, Gardening and Land Programs, and Adventure Program), and our creative expressive therapies (Art Therapy and Sandtray Therapy). Finally, Chapter 7 concludes with a view to the path ahead.

As you work your way through the book, you will find yourself continually reminded of the leap of faith, the perseverance through hard times and good times, the unwavering adherence to core values – all that it has taken humanly and in the spirit to establish and sustain this foundation. You'll find these same values and spirit reflected in the material drawn from staff's writings and interviews. You'll find them woven into the land and buildings that house what Wellspring and its Arch Bridge School have become. Taken together, as a body of hope, the Wellspring of today lives and extends this legacy.

Dan Murray, Psy.D.

Wellspring's Chief Executive Officer

CHAPTER 1

THE FOUNDATION — WELLSPRING'S MISSION, PHILOSOPHY, AND VALUES

Place was important to us.

We wanted our treatment center to be a home, a nurturing place where the care of body included the care of land, plants and animals, as well as people.

THE DISCOVERY

Written by Phyllis Beauvais, Ph.D.

In September 1977, while praying and searching for the right place to found Wellspring, I was driving with our real estate agent, George Brower, after looking at perhaps the tenth decidedly inappropriate piece of property. Feeling a bit discouraged, I wondered if we would ever find what we needed. As we drove down from the top of Arch Bridge Road, I looked over to the right, and saw a beautiful old house and barn nestled among the hills. At that moment, shafts of sunlight suddenly broke through the clouds and illuminated it, and I felt a rush of response.

"That's it!" I said to George, "That's the place I have in mind." He laughed and said, "Good luck. That will never happen. The man who owns that property loves it dearly and he will never sell." Although the image still haunted me, I tried to let it go. Two days later I got a call from George, saying, "You won't believe this, but the man who owns that property on Arch Bridge Road has just been transferred. He has to leave immediately, and he is putting the house on the market."

We went there at once, signed our offer on September 18th, and on October 15th, Richard and I moved in with our children, Cassandra and Joel. We also brought goats, which we had because Cassandra was passionate about animals.

Place was important to us. We wanted our treatment center to be a home, a nurturing place where the care of body included the care of land, plants, and animals, as well as people. We were lay oblates of the Abbey of Regina Laudis – a Benedictine women's monastery located in Bethlehem, Connecticut – and our Benedictine roots had imbued our spirituality with a reverence for the created matter of the earth. We wanted the place to embody that reverence. And we wanted to attract an extraordinary staff, both professionally sophisticated and also earthy enough to risk living the personal and relational values of our philosophy.

This book is about that philosophy and our work to embody it. It begins with our touchstone: a statement of Wellspring's mission, treatment philosophy, and core values.

MISSION STATEMENT, TREATMENT PHILOSOPHY, AND CORE VALUES

Wellspring is a therapeutic and educational center dedicated to healing and learning through relational approaches – to self, others, creation, and Spirit – which touch and bring forth the *wellspring* of personal being unique to each individual, giving hope to each person and family in our care.

Four core values are at the heart of Wellspring's philosophy and approach to treatment and education: *Personal, relational, intensive and comprehensive*. To the degree that these values infuse our practice, Wellspring's uniqueness and strength as a healing agency will be sustained.

PERSONAL

Psychiatry addresses psychopathology through differential diagnosis based on the symptoms and etiology of emotional and behavioral disorders. But awareness of the individual as *person* is even more fundamental to treatment and education, because it pertains to the individual's essential nature – to a quality of *personal being* that is inherent, unique and imbued with spirit. This uniqueness is apparent in a child's basic disposition and giftedness – something evident at birth to any mother or father – something that becomes more and more wondrously revealed as the child grows.

Because the essential nature of an individual is inherent, it is imbued with *spirit* partaking in the greater mystery of Being. The sacredness and dignity of each person is rooted in this spiritual dimension and resides in each individual as the *wellspring* of a true identity. However, personal essence is but the seed of *personhood*, not its realization or fulfillment: that is a lifelong process. Our job is to recognize, uncover and disclose this seed, to protect and nourish it, so that the individual can align with it consciously as the basis for a positive identity and creative life.

What distinguishes Wellspring as an agency is the intentional awareness, reverence and respect that we hold from this perspective for each individual in our care. If pathology is thought of as accrued layers that cover and distort this core of personhood, our efforts to work through defenses and unconscious beliefs about self and others also involve the perception, mirroring, affirmation and support of this personal core. How a staff member can best support this process is by becoming known to himself as person, so he can be a window for another through relationship.

RELATIONAL

Our basic assumption is that the wounds of emotional disorder were developed through relationships; therefore, *relationship* must also be the primary medium for healing. A commitment to the *personal*, coupled with clinical understanding and good practice, is what will ground our approach. What we must strive for is relationship that proceeds from an "I-

Thou" orientation (Buber, 1958), rather than from an "I-It" attitude, where the *other* is related to as object.

At Wellspring we need to manage and confront pathological and self-destructive behavior, but our more basic effort will be to help the individual develop a healthy relationship to self and others, which goes beyond behavior management alone. Sartre says, "Hell is other people," because there is no exit, no escape from *them*. While treatment at Wellspring may feel like hell at times for clients and for staff, what will release us from the hell of *others* is how we relate to one another. The way through this human predicament is imaged by a traditional Vietnamese parable:

> PEOPLE IN HELL ARE GIVEN CHOPSTICKS A YARD LONG, SO THEY CANNOT FEED THEMSELVES THOUGH THEY ARE DESPERATELY HUNGRY. PEOPLE IN HEAVEN ARE GIVEN THE SAME SIZED CHOPSTICKS, BUT THEY CHOOSE TO FEED ONE ANOTHER.

Symptoms evolve as substitute ways of meeting unmet needs. Defenses serve to protect the individual, despite their pathological nature and destructive effects. The problem for a healing process is how to effect a transition – a transformation – that meets the same basic needs but in healthier ways. This is a vulnerable process – a desert of unknowing – as an individual struggles to give up ways that have worked (often with terrible effects) and tries out ways never risked before. Given the nature and severity of emotional injury, much is required of the individual and staff persons who engage in this mutually healing process.

What we must do, in and through relationship, is imaged by the way a lobster acquires a new shell when it has outgrown its old one. While the lobster sheds its shell, exposing its vulnerable body, it must find a safe place – a refuge, perhaps under a rock – and remain there until its tender flesh forms a new shell. Wellspring must become that safe place, that holding body, to bring about such a healing transformation.

The first requirement is to build a container and create a culture of safety and trust. What we attempt to bring forth for the individual within this enclosure is the ability to be *real* – to be true to oneself, authentic, self-assertive, expressive, and able to receive and give love and support. Emotional acceptance, validation and empathy through attunement to feeling is what will encourage and sustain this development. Facing oneself "in the eyes and hearts of others" must be combined with finding oneself as seen, mirrored, and affirmed as a *person* of value. Learning the skills of relationship – caring confrontation and feedback, relational dialogue, emotional regulation and conflict resolution – teaches one how to be effective while living in the ongoing tension of human relationship.

A dimension of our *relational* work that cannot be emphasized enough is *relationship to body* – especially to how one's body is rooted in the *Body of Creation*. In this respect, Wellspring sets itself against the current cultural drift – that pervasive tendency to relate to body as *object*, rather than as embodied *being*. An early Wellspring brochure states:

> WELLSPRING TEACHES HONEST ATTENTION TO PROCESS. WORK WITH SOIL, PLANTS, ANIMALS AND MATERIALS, AS WELL AS WITH PEOPLE, BRINGS FORTH A DEEP SENSE OF THE VALUE OF CREATION ESSENTIAL TO HEALING.
>
> IF A PERSON IS AWAKENED INTO CONSCIOUS RELATIONSHIP WITH THE MATTER OF CREATION, THEN THE PROCESS OF WORK WITH THE CONCRETE REALITIES OF PLANT, ANIMAL, AND HUMAN BODIES BECOMES HEALING.

Personal essence is revealed through action – especially through the instinctive ways of response that are apparent in manual work, animal care, horticulture, and adventure program – side-by-side, body-to-body experience. These contexts and activities are too easily dismissed as "chores," rather than cherished as *windows of experience for revealing the personal*. Without this consciousness (which staff may not have been privileged to develop before coming to Wellspring), we fall victim to the drift we are presently immersed in by our culture, where body becomes reified as *object*, but is progressively stripped of *being* as subject, becoming more and more buried by virtual reality.

TREATMENT AS INTENSIVE

Intensive treatment goes "deep," rather than staying on the behavioral surface, in an effort to reach and resolve the fundamental aspects of a disorder. In so doing, the treatment context must be able to hold what is risked and made vulnerable in the healing process. It is this marriage of *masculine activation and feminine holding* that becomes the guiding principle of intensive treatment: open only what you, the client and the situation can hold and integrate. What this requires is *attunement* to the individual in process and knowledge of one's own and the treatment team's capacity and limits in taking on this responsibility. Transformation takes time – not just waiting, but time as brave persistence in the calibrated steps of preparation, readiness for exposure, release and integration.

At Wellspring, we have always sought out and explored approaches that have this intensive capacity. Safe, healing touch, emotional expressive work, attachment therapy and the *therapeutic use of personality* are cases in point.

It is not technique *per se* or a particular method that makes an approach suitable for Wellspring. Innovative methods require a continual sorting out through experience – evaluating each of them in the light of our values, our willingness to try something out, seeing what works and what doesn't, while holding to professional ethics and the ABCs of good mothering and fathering.

TREATMENT AS COMPREHENSIVE

Because each individual is unique and multi-dimensional, treatment at Wellspring strives to be holistic, able to engage the whole person – body, mind, heart and spirit. Because emotional disorders are complex, treatment must be multi-modal, having the capacity to address different aspects of a person and a disorder simultaneously.

Wellspring's programs strive to combine analytic, cognitive-behavioral, family systems, interpersonal-interactive, emotional-expressive, creative-expressive, and body-experiential modalities in a coordinated way. Treatment planning must also be collaboratively convergent – able to focus and coordinate different modalities in a concerted way upon a given treatment issue. In therapy with attachment difficulties, for example, expressive work has been integrated with family work. Sensory integration and neurofeedback training have been used to address neurological impairment and brain-state imbalance. Each modality contributes in its own way to the goal of improving emotional self-regulation and building the heart-to-heart connections necessary for bonding and attachment.

The goal of treatment and treatment planning is for different modalities and providers to work together in a convergent, synergistic way, rather than as independent, parallel islands of intervention. Treatment that is convergent and synergistic is simply more powerful.

THE WELLSPRING LOGO – A SYMBOL OF WELLSPRING'S VALUES

Personal, relational, intensive and *comprehensive* – these four values are the cornerstones of Wellspring's treatment philosophy and approach. The heart of this philosophy is the *person in relationship*, starting with one's own *person* in relationship to another.

This is illustrated by Wellspring's Logo, which is a mandala – a square of four quarters that appears in many spiritual traditions as a symbolic image of wholeness, the integrated fullness of human being. A mandala is also thought to image the divine presence in our lives.

The rich colors of golden ochre, turquoise, rust and blue reflect the primal elements of Creation – earth, air, fire and water. The curves and angles, swirls and structures, express the constant interplay of the Yin and the Yang, the feminine and masculine energies of receptivity and activation fundamental to creative life.

At the center of the logo is a circle that images the Well from which we draw our name. The Well reaches down into the earth to the wellspring, source of living water. This expresses our belief that within each individual there is a wellspring of personal being, unique, unrepeatable in essence and imbued with spirit. As source of the sacredness and dignity of each individual, this wellspring within links us to one another and to all of Creation.

The Well is centered by a cross. As symbol, the cross juxtaposes two contrasting dimensions of life – the vertical and the horizontal. These represent two pathways of personal growth and participation in a more inclusive way of human being. The vertical line is the line of the Spirit, extending downwards into the depths of Being and upwards to its transcendent heights. The horizontal line extends outwards to the ends of the earth – into the world of body and relationship. Through relationship we become the arms of the cross, opening our small selves to embrace humanity. This is the work of Wellspring.

CHAPTER 2

THE HISTORY OF WELLSPRING

Beneath the historical surface of its starting point, the conception of Wellspring was like any other – a moment in time, a place where genealogical lines converge, and where among all possible events that could have taken place, this one did.

ORIGINS OF WELLSPRING'S PHILOSOPHY AND VALUES

A true history is more than a factual chronicle of events leading up to the present. It is also a revelation – an uncovering in retrospect – of the archetypal underpinnings that have shaped and given meaning to these events. The history of Wellspring, written in this way, joins fact and causality to that deeper, more mysterious process of becoming, allowing us to image this dynamic of growth into the future.

We founded Wellspring in September of 1977. We had come to an impasse at The Country Place, a residential treatment center for young adults, where Richard had worked since its inception in 1965 and Phyllis had joined him in 1970. We were a couple, seven years married, discovering our own approach to healing. Our apprenticeship as psychotherapists had been completed, and though we had much, much more to learn, with vision and dedication we needed our own situation to carry this out.

Beneath the historical surface of its starting point, the conception of Wellspring was like any other – a moment in time, a place where genealogical lines converge, spirit leaps and takes on flesh, and where among all possible events that could have taken place, this one did. But unlike a river, which has no choice but to accept whatever meets and joins with it, founders are able to select and choose those tributaries resonant with their own vision, to "marry" those that complement and enhance that vision, while letting go of those that don't.

Many individuals, each a *wellspring* in their own right, drawing in turn upon other wellsprings, have become tributaries to the river of this foundation. Others are still to come. It is important that this history name and give credit to some of these sources, but it is even more important for the future of Wellspring to appreciate the creative dynamism, the receptivity and discernment in the Spirit that has been our way of embracing and integrating old and new ways that contribute to the work.

Did we have a plan for what Wellspring would be or become? No, that was never our way. We improvised with the resources we had, meeting as creatively as we could what we faced at any point along the way. Our process was more unplanned and fortuitous, where intention mingled with daily step-by-step immersion in the work, responding to what was here and now, as well as whatever came to meet us on the way.

The "miracle" of Wellspring is that it has survived and flourished, and while some might laud us for vision and tenacity, this is true mostly in retrospect. It is important to state for the future that in the most important sense Wellspring has never been under our control. Like any child, or any destiny, we simply met what unfolded before us, holding fast to our values and intention to heal, living under the subtle and sometimes heavy-handed guidance of the Spirit, making the best use we could of the resources at hand.

Born of a farm family in western Nebraska, Phyllis came to this work as an accomplished poet, with a background in philosophy, literature, and experimental theater. A Roman Catholic upbringing, with its emphasis on service, led Phyllis to the Catholic Worker, where for a time she was secretary to Dorothy Day, while working in a soup kitchen on the Bowery. This strongly spiritual disposition led her to active involvement in the Gurdjieff work, and from there to intensive meditation. Involvement in SAT (Seekers After Truth), an eclectic approach developed by Claudio Naranjo, M.D., amplified Phyllis's experience of meditation and exposed her to the spiritual practices and psychological treasures of many traditions. SAT and its relation to Sufism became the subject of Phyllis's doctoral dissertation. From 1970 to 1977, Phyllis worked at The Country Place as a psychotherapist in training under the supervisory direction of Renee Nell, a noted Jungian therapist known for her special gift in dream interpretation.

Richard brought to this union and to Wellspring the unconscious legacy of his maternal grandparents, who were missionaries in Africa for 40 years. He was also an athlete, a swimmer, whose love of the body extended to a love of manual work and the dance. His early graduate studies at the University of California-Berkeley were in the History of Ideas, which gave ample opportunity to pursue his passion for literature, art, poetry and music. It also led him to Jungian psychology and psychotherapy, where his intensive training with Renee Nell at The Country Place also gave him a deep awareness that the work of healing required a spiritual grounding that a humanistic orientation alone could not provide. At Daytop Village and The Country Place, Richard's dedication to service became rooted in profound experiences of the healing power of therapeutic community, which led him directly to the co-creation of Wellspring.

Wellspring's "family tree" originates with its founders, who brought into union not only their personal histories but different lines of experience with healing. Richard's line was rooted in his experience of Daytop, The Country Place and Jungian Psychotherapy: Phyllis's with the Catholic Worker, the Gurdjieff Work, the art of expressive meditation, theater, and the art of poetry. These lines were first wedded at The Country Place, but they became spiritually grounded through oblation to the Abbey of Regina Laudis, a community of contemplative Benedictine women.

DAYTOP

Wellspring was founded as a residential therapeutic community, and one of our "parents" in this model was Daytop, a residential treatment center for drug addiction established in the early 1960s as a pilot project of the Kings County Probation Department. Daytop was born of Synanon, the breakthrough treatment for heroin addiction, which Daniel Casriel, M.D. has described in his book, *So Fair a House* (1963). While Synanon's leadership and direction became increasingly problematic, leading to its eventual demise, Daytop flourished over the years to become the training center for other substance abuse residential treatment centers throughout the world.

Richard became involved with Daytop through his friendship with David Deitsch, who took over as Program Director in 1963 after leaving Synanon. The Daytop experience was a profound exposure to the healing power of an intense, confrontational mode of therapeutic community, run by ex-addicts and centered around the Encounter Group, an innovative treatment approach at that time. At Daytop's 40th anniversary celebration, Richard described his experience:

> I WAS NOT AN ADDICT AND WAS NEVER ATTRACTED TO DRUGS, BUT MY LIFE WAS IN SERIOUS CRISIS... I HAD NO IDEA WHAT TO DO WITH IT AND WAS COMPLETELY STUCK, SEEING NO WAY OUT, NO WAY BACK, AND NO WAY TO MOVE FORWARD. DAYTOP NOT ONLY CHANGED MY LIFE; IT MAY HAVE SAVED IT.
>
> IN THE ENCOUNTER GROUPS EVERY ASPECT OF MY TROUBLED LIFE AND PERSONALITY WAS CONFRONTED. THESE WERE PEER GROUPS IN THE TRUEST SENSE OF THE WORD: NO ONE WAS EXEMPT FROM ENCOUNTER BY FUNCTION OR POSITION. EVERYONE WAS EQUAL – EQUALLY ON THE "HOT SEAT" AND EQUALLY VULNERABLE. NO LIMIT WAS SET TO RAW EMOTIONAL EXPRESSION, AND ANYTHING SHORT OF PHYSICAL VIOLENCE WAS PERMITTED. EVERYONE IN THE GROUP WAS A KIND OF THERAPIST, IN THAT EACH INDIVIDUAL SPOKE THEIR EMOTIONAL TRUTH, AND THE PERSON ON THE "HOT SEAT" HAD TO DEAL WITH IT. I MARVELED AT THE KEEN PERCEPTION AND AWARENESS OF THESE STREET-SMART EXTRAORDINARY PEOPLE, WHO LITERALLY TORE THROUGH INTELLECTUALIZATION AND WERE IMPOSSIBLE TO CON. HARD AS IT WAS, I LOVED THE INTENSITY AND REALNESS OF THE PROCESS – THE STRIPPING DOWN OF ANY BULLSHIT TO ITS RAW EMOTIONAL CORE.

David Deitsch was a charismatic and inspirational leader deeply committed to the work. He seemed aware of each individual and every situation that affected the community, and would leave no stone unturned to address it. David's concept of "recovery" extended beyond becoming "clean" of drugs to a vision of personal growth for each individual that offered a way to full citizenship in the human family. The way to achieve this was through active participation in a community of responsibility and care for one another. Daytop provided such a community.

What Richard learned at Daytop were basic principles of therapeutic community that became part of Wellspring's heritage. The first was a belief that each individual, staff or client, possesses an intrinsic therapeutic capacity that could be mobilized and brought to bear in the healing process. In the intimate and intense relational milieu of a residential community, the *therapeutic use of personality* would become a cornerstone of Wellspring's approach to treatment. Living together and working closely with clients in a residential milieu, there is no place to hide. To engage in a relationally focused treatment process, one must strive first of all to be authentically oneself.

A second principle is that everyone in the community must be an engaged participant in the therapeutic process. Walk the walk, don't just talk the talk. Whatever you expect from clients, be accountable for in yourself. With no one exempt by function or position, the encounter group was an effective clearing house for interpersonal conflicts and community issues. At Wellspring the focus would be on caring confrontation, caring feedback, staying in the tension, and bringing in a third person to address whatever issues might arise between staff and resident and staff and staff. These processes would keep the fabric of community life from being eroded by cliques, silent enmities, and festering conflicts.

A third principle was that commitment to treatment should be tested prior to admission and at different points along the way, but particularly after an individual had gone absent without leave (AWOL) or had bailed out of treatment. At Wellspring, we require the screening process with clients and families to be up-front and exacting about the work that will be required of each. A clear commitment to engage in treatment is expected, and return to the community from an AWOL should never be made easy.

At Daytop, mountains were made out of molehills, because seemingly insignificant behaviors reveal underlying attitudes that need to be addressed. To avoid confronting an individual's behavior, however petty that might seem, would place the resident in greater danger. If he could con the staff or get away with something, even something small, he would not be safe from himself in the future. Heroin addiction was truly a life and death matter, which gave special meaning to this principle. But a resident at Wellspring also needs to know that the "parents" are always one step ahead of her and smart enough and strong enough to take care of her.

"Acting as if" was another core therapeutic practice at Daytop. Nathan Glaser's book, *Reality Therapy*, was born of this approach. By engaging in externally healthy behavior, without insisting on sincerity of motivation, core feelings could be catalyzed to reveal patterns of identity and self-image that needed to be changed. Within the enclosure of the therapeutic community, new roles and new patterns of behavior could be taken on from this "as if" perspective that could build confidence in a positive identity for the future.

Finally, Daytop demonstrated through its success in treating severe addiction, that professionally trained clinicians have only a partial answer to problems. What is of equal importance is personal experience and a personal relationship to the problem in order to know what is needed for healing. In this respect, the role of peers and coverage staff at Wellspring is as important, and more so in some ways, as that of professional clinicians.

It was at Daytop in 1964 during a weekend seminar with Abraham Maslow that Richard re-encountered Renee Nell, a noted Jungian therapist, who was an invited guest. Richard had been a client of Renee's for six months before he became involved with Daytop, and she had come there to learn what it would take to develop a residential center for psychiatric patients. Renee and Richard renewed their acquaintance, and she invited him to become a co-therapist in her groups in Manhattan with the goal of adapting the confrontational approach of the Encounter Group to the needs of her clients. In the following year, Renee would start a residential center for psychiatric patients in Connecticut called The Country Place – the direct forerunner of Wellspring.

THE PHILOSOPHY (NO REFUGE) – POEM AUTHORED BY RICHARD BEAUVAIS

Before Richard left Daytop to join Renee, David Deitsch asked him to write a new "philosophy" for Daytop to replace the old version adopted from Synanon. While walking the beach on Staten Island musing about his Daytop experience, the lines of a poem came to him. He wrote them down that day while traveling on the ferry back to Manhattan. This simple poem has become an integral part of Wellspring's treatment philosophy.

"No Refuge" – by Richard Beauvais, Ph.D.

I am here, because there is no refuge,
Finally, from myself.
Until I confront myself in the eyes
And hearts of others,
I am running.

Until I suffer them to share my secrets,
I have no safety from them.
Afraid to be known, I can know
Neither myself nor any other --
I will be alone.

Where else but in our common ground
Can I find such a mirror?
Here, together, I can at last appear
Clearly to myself,

Not as the giant of my dreams,
Nor the dwarf of my fears,
But as myself – part of a whole –
With my share in its purpose.

In this ground we can each take root
And grow.
Not alone anymore as in death,
But alive to ourselves and to others.

In 2005, at the World Conference of Therapeutic Communities hosted by Daytop in New York City, Richard was honored as the author of "The Philosophy" at a reception held at the United Nations. Representatives from more than 50 nations were present at the event and many of these had adopted "The Philosophy" for their Residential Treatment Centers throughout the world. The poem has been translated into more than 30 different languages.

THE COUNTRY PLACE

In the spring of 1964, Renee Nell visited Daytop with the intention to develop a residential center for psychiatric patients. She had been seeing many clients in her private practice, who needed more intensive treatment than outpatient services could provide, but would not benefit from extended hospital stays. For therapy to be effective with this population, Renee believed it needed to draw upon the day-to-day experience of living and working together in a therapeutically focused residential community.

Renee Nell was an extraordinary woman, a German Jewish immigrant who had fought in the resistance against Hitler and later came to America to escape the Holocaust. She was a vital and creative person who became a Hollywood script writer while simultaneously training at the Jung Institutes in Los Angeles and Zurich to become an analyst. From there, she settled in New York and established a flourishing private practice.

In the late spring of 1965, Renee leased an old country inn in Warren, Connecticut, and called it The Country Place. Based on its initial success, Renee proceeded in 1967 to purchase a 50-acre property from the Montfort Sisters in Litchfield, Connecticut, as a permanent home. The property had several buildings, including a mansion equipped with a greenhouse, stables that became converted into a dormitory, a small farmhouse and two large barns.

Richard began work at The Country Place in 1965, while attending City College for a Masters Degree in Clinical Psychology. Two years later, he enrolled in a doctoral program in Community Social Psychology at Boston College, while continuing to work at The Country Place on weekends and summers. In 1970, he returned to work there full-time as Assistant Clinical Director to Renee. While in Boston, Richard renewed his relationship with Phyllis Masek, whom he had met earlier in California during the summer of 1967. Phyllis joined Richard at The Country Place in 1970 with her daughter Cassandra, working first as Renee's secretary and soon after as a therapist in training. We were married in October of that year.

At The Country Place, Richard matured as a therapist with Renee as his mentor. He had always loved fairy tales, mythology, and the dream world, and became skilled at dream interpretation under Renee's tutelage. Art Therapy (painting from the unconscious) became one of his favorite therapeutic activities. He also learned about the art of Work Therapy and how the residential milieu could be focused on the development of relational skills and self-expression. While learning the craft of individual therapy, Phyllis was given the freedom to develop her own style and skills as a group therapist and, particularly, as an emotional expressive therapist. At The Country Place, the creative-expressive therapies of art therapy, dance therapy and ceramic arts were used for self exploration and self-expression.

What we learned most from Renee through our experience at The Country Place was that residential treatment could be done *in our own way*, based on our own values, and proceeding from the marriage of our complementary therapeutic charisms. She proved that it was not only possible but even advantageous to work outside of the medical establishment, while maintaining relationship with it. All it would take to do so would be guts, fortitude, the right kind of humility – and the grace of God.

JUNGIAN PSYCHOLOGY

Among other things, Renee Nell opened to us the rich world of Jungian psychology and dream interpretation, which offer such a textured way of understanding the structure and dynamics of the psyche and the role of the *unconscious* in everyday life. We brought that understanding to Wellspring.

Part of Jung's appeal to us was the bridge he provided between psychology and spirituality through his understanding of the archetypal dimension of symbolic thought. This proved important for our involvement with the Abbey of Regina Laudis, which had a working familiarity with Jungian concepts in the context of community life. Although Jungian Psychology was never in the foreground of our work at Wellspring, it gave depth and meaning to the multi-modal, holistic approach to treatment we adopted from The Country Place and developed further on our own.

Jung conceived of the psyche as a dynamically interrelated system of component parts; most notably, the *ego, shadow, persona, anima* and *animus*. Dreams reflected the inner workings of the psyche in response to what was important or pressing in the dreamer's life. They did this from the standpoint of the *unconscious*, which balanced or compensated what was lacking or extreme in the dreamer's conscious attitude. As a window into tendencies and motivations outside of subjective awareness, dream interpretation was a medium for depth psychology in our relational approach.

Awareness of *shadow* qualities in the individual was particularly useful in this respect. *Shadow* was a term Jung used to characterize what was undeveloped in the personality, or qualities the individual suppressed and kept in the dark to himself and others. But *shadow* elements were also sources of growth if these qualities could be integrated in a positive way. By seeing the strength inherent in a negative behavior, work with *shadow* would become an important dimension of treatment. Learning how to channel suppressed or indirect anger into positive self-assertion and empowerment is a case in point.

Shadow is dynamically related to the *persona*, the Greek word for the mask used in dramatic productions. *Persona* represents how we present ourselves to the world and like to think of ourselves. While *persona* is our Dr. Jekyll, *shadow* is our Mr. Hyde. Taken together, they offer a more three-dimensional view of the personality, focusing treatment on the work of mutual integration. A person who presents a constant "happy face" to the world, for instance, would be challenged to drop it and allow her actual feelings to emerge, making her self-presentation more integral and authentic.

Jung's concepts of *psychological masculinity and femininity* were another aspect of his psychology that gave depth to our relational approach. Distinct from gender and social roles, psychological masculinity and femininity represent contrasting modes of being – ways of action and interaction in everyone, male or female. If both masculinity and femininity are developed, the person is more balanced and whole, with increased capacity for relationship. To be able to assert oneself and also be receptive to others is a case in point. More often than not, however, either masculinity or femininity is developed at the expense of the other, leading to imbalance and relational problems. Nevertheless, the undeveloped side will still be operative, while functioning in a more primitive and problematic way.

Jung's system of *psychological types* was also useful to us, because it provided insight into persons and relationships in terms of *individual differences*. Based on the attitudes of extraversion and introversion and the four functions of thinking, feeling, intuition and sense perception, people were distinguished from one another by their differing gifts. The Myers-Briggs Test, widely used in Human Resources, is based on Jung's system. The study of psychological types provided a way of seeing people dynamically in relationship, because individuals gifted in one way of knowing or perceiving are *ipso facto* limited in its counterpart. For example, a person developed in thinking will tend to be deficient in feeling and vice versa. Because superiority in one aspect typically is coupled with inferiority in its opposite, no individual is ever complete unto himself, which is why we need each other in a working community.

Understanding how different types functioned and interacted was very helpful in therapeutic work, especially in couple counseling and family work. But it was also important for work relationships at Wellspring. Because our natural tendency is to expect other people to function as we do, we are surprised to find out that they don't. They simply know and do things differently. This can be an ongoing source of frustration and conflict, which an understanding of type differences and how to bridge these differences could help clarify and resolve. In Wellspring's early days, we provided training to staff in *psychological types* as a way of building community consciousness.

Jung also emphasized the importance of the creative-expressive therapies, because the *self* is often manifested through the creative act. This had special appeal to us, because of our personal interests in poetry, art, music and dance. At one time, along with art therapy and dance therapy, we included puppetry, music therapy, clay therapy and drama improvisation.

Later, we added Jungian Sandtray Therapy – discussed in Chapter 6 – to the programmatic mix. When we began treating adolescents, however, school requirements filled much of the daily schedule, forcing us to cut back on our creative-expressive offerings.

Jung's final contribution to our founding philosophy was his conception of personality development as purposive, positing an inherent press from within to become oneself. This resonated with our belief in the inherent *wellspring* of personal being in every individual. The challenge was to see, mirror and affirm this inner *wellspring*, so that it could become the basis for a truly personal identity and creative life. This concept was also linked with healing. We had often witnessed, particularly through emotional expressive work, how the body seems to know in some mysterious way what it needs for healing, whether this knowing is conscious or not. We encouraged our therapists to attune to and facilitate this inner treatment plan, which links healing to the process of becoming more and more fully oneself.

The training in Jungian Psychology we received from Renee Nell at The Country Place provided a bridge for us to begin the work of Wellspring. When we encountered the Abbey of Regina Laudis, we were ready to take our Jungian understanding of the relationship between psychology and spirituality to greater depths.

THE ABBEY OF REGINA LAUDIS

Although we shared a Roman Catholic upbringing, both of us had withdrawn from active participation in the Church, although we continued to develop our spirituality by exploring other traditions and meditation practice. At The Country Place, Richard had become increasingly aware of a need for a deeper spiritual grounding than a humanistic orientation alone could provide, if only to counteract the burnout that comes from living the unrelenting intensity of therapeutic community life. Quite fortuitously, this led us to the Abbey of Regina Laudis, a contemplative Benedictine monastery for women in Bethlehem, Connecticut.

In the early 1970s, the Abbey had become actively engaged in fostering lay spiritual communities, which were more or less organized around personal *charism* and professional call. We were attracted by the spiritual and intellectual vitality of the Abbey, which offered fertile ground for what we were seeking. Regina Laudis spirituality was grounded in the *mystery of the incarnation*, which was embodied outwardly in the care of land, plants, animals and interpersonal relationship. Work and prayer – *ora et labora* – was the credo of Benedictine monastic life, which was coupled with a mandate by Pope Paul VI for each nun to become developed in her secular profession either before or after entering monastic life. The

Abbey's familiarity with Jungian concepts, particularly the dynamic interplay of psychological masculinity and femininity in relationship, made it immediately attractive to us both.

Shortly after we began relating to the Abbey, we joined with several other lay professionals to form a group we called The Healing Community. In 1977, with four other members of this group, we purchased a 300-acre parcel of land known as Three Rivers Farm in Bridgewater, Connecticut, at the confluence of the Shepaug and Housatonic Rivers. Our intention was to found an ecologically-focused ecumenical center for the development of lay spirituality and personal mission. We called it *Promisek*, after its Native American name on the original deed, meaning "Land He Walks on Forever." In order to more authentically live the healing mission inspired by this new commitment, we decided to leave The Country Place and found our own treatment center. Wellspring was born of this leap of faith. Quite separately from Wellspring, Promisek has continued to live and to grow, nourishing us and others as a contemplative grounding for our professional call. Through the medium of the Healing Community, and in ongoing relationship with the Abbey, we engaged in an intensive process of spiritual formation that provided the ground upon which Wellspring was founded and grew. Values we held about the *person* and *relationship* from humanistic psychology gained greater depth and meaning from this experience. Values about land, manual work, and the care of plants and animals, which became integral to Wellspring's treatment philosophy and approach, were developed through this exposure to Benedictine life. The most profound impact on the development of Wellspring, however, was an understanding of what would constitute the lifeblood of the therapeutic community we were struggling to found.

Under the direction of Lady Abbess, Mother Benedict Duss, OSB, the Abbey held a profound respect for the inherent uniqueness of each individual, expressed in terms of one's essential nature and giftedness. What a surprise it was to discover that community life at the Abbey was based on the honoring of *essential difference*; and that it was the development of the individual and not conformity that the Abbey was dedicated to bring forth. Because difference is also at the root of relational conflict, commitment to personal development was coupled with ways of addressing and resolving conflict. Try to imagine forty educated and professionally developed women living interdependently under the same roof! This was both spirituality and psychology made real in the relational friction of community life. On a larger scale, it paralleled what Phyllis and I were working out within the crucible of our own marital relationship as we struggled to hold and develop Wellspring, Promisek and our own family.

The Abbey had an understanding of psychological masculinity and femininity that went far beyond anything we had known, because it was perceived as a dynamic underlying all of creation and lived out within the crucible of relationship in every aspect of community life. The Abbey's focus on *complementarity* as basic to creative life influenced how we looked at our own relationship and the dynamics of leadership at Wellspring. We sought to establish male-female complement relationships wherever possible, while addressing the psychologically masculine and feminine dimensions of these relationships, and attending to the balance between structure and nurture.

The spiritual underpinning of community life at the Abbey was based on *humility* – the backbone of *The Holy Rule of St. Benedict.* Humility is derived from *humus*, which means to be in or from the earth – which starts with being grounded in both one's gifts and limitations. If *who I am is also who I am not* – meaning my giftedness is inseparable from what I also lack, then the essence of community life is based ultimately on how we need one another, and how the unity of a working community is achieved through the synergy of its parts. This depends, in part, upon each member's ability to exercise their individual gifts within the context of their work, so we consciously sought out what staff persons were passionate about in their lives, and encouraged them to incorporate these interests into treatment-related modalities. The broad range of therapeutic modalities we introduced grew first from this cultivation of staff interests; professional training and certification would come later.

At the Abbey, self-giving also meant becoming a *servant* to the whole, which meant being in service to others in their personal becoming. The continual work of self-giving and the process of self-transformation at the heart of the Abbey's spiritual life became a model for what we aspired to at Wellspring. Our life commitment to each other, to the Healing Community, to Promisek and to Wellspring became crucibles for grinding our personal egocentricities into committed love.

Where Renee Nell had been master to us in Jungian Psychology and the art of psychotherapy, Lady Abbess became spiritual master to us in the work of sustaining Wellspring. Before becoming a monastic, Lady Abbess had been a Sorbonne trained physician and surgeon. The fact that each nun had been operative in a particular profession before entering the Abbey, before becoming a contemplative, was an important asset to our work. The opportunity to meet regularly with one of the sisters, who held a contemplative awareness while also understanding the nature and challenges of clinical work, was an invaluable resource and formative experience for us. It provided a necessary *overview*, so to speak, when more often than not we could see only what was in front of our face.

A contemplative viewpoint involves the ability to listen and be open to the guidance of the Spirit, which could come through many different doorways easy to miss. As we look back in retrospect, Wellspring made many wise choices through the years that have helped it to survive and flourish where other residential centers have failed. This was due in part to holding with integrity to the core values at the heart of our mission, while resisting the temptations of expediency. But above all it was the guidance of the Spirit that was the star we set ourselves to follow.

Finally, the faith dimension of our commitments provided us with the backbone that sustained us through the many difficult times we faced as Wellspring developed. Living at Wellspring with our children through the first year was very difficult. Later, having to come in to deal with crises at any hour of the night was exhausting. And we faced the constant challenge of walking a financial tightrope from day one to the present. Now we look back and wonder how we could have done it...and yet we did, through the efforts of many, many others in addition to our own. Through it all, the support that came to us from within will stand as the enduring mystery of this foundation. Much as we struggled and suffered, to which anyone who takes on this work will attest, we can only say we were blessed.

A BRIEF CHRONOLOGICAL HISTORY

After founding Wellspring in 1977, we lived for the first year as houseparents in what is now Beauvais House with our children, Cassandra and Joel, and Wellspring's first four young adult residents. Joseph and Susan Braccio took over as houseparents the next year, followed by Ben and Micheline Lockerd for the year and a half after that. From these humble beginnings, Wellspring has grown during the course of more than four decades to encompass five separate programs located on two campuses – employing dozens of professionals and, over time, serving thousands of children, adolescents, adults, and families. During this time, we have been blessed by a succession of Chief Executive Officers, Boards of Directors, and staff who have given themselves tirelessly to Wellspring's continuing growth and development. Much remains yet to be written in the history of Wellspring in the decades to come; what follows is a brief chronicle of these first four decades of this evolving foundation.

1977 TO 1994

Phyllis served as Wellspring's first CEO from 1977 to 1994. This was not a position she sought, but in the beginning we were a tiny organization, and she was best equipped for the job. She was a natural leader and an actress, with the ability to adapt herself to whatever the role required. Throughout her years of service, she gave herself fully to it.

Phyllis focused initially on the development of the personal and relational approach to treatment that is Wellspring's trademark. Born in Nebraska from a farming background, Phyllis was both earthy and artistic. Work with animals and soil, hearth and home, the creative and expressive arts, was an extension of her personality and giftedness. As poet, animal lover, gardener, therapist and mother, Phyllis was the soil from which Wellspring grew. She was also the first in Wellspring's line of CEOs that would blend therapeutic and management skills in some degree of balance. Throughout her tenure, Phyllis conducted our Expressive Therapy groups in every Wellspring program.

In 1981, Wellspring became licensed by the State of Connecticut Department of Health as an Intermediate Treatment Facility. This was a unique designation at the time shared only by The Country Place. What distinguished Wellspring from a traditional halfway house was our commitment to intensive treatment, which continues to characterize our niche to this day within the residential spectrum. The Intermediate Treatment Facility license was an important step forward, but also presented us with a major problem to surmount. It required Wellspring to maintain 24/7 nursing coverage, a significant financial burden for such a tiny facility. So, we shifted from our original house-parenting model to create space for more residents and expanded our census from six to eight.

Wellspring's Board of Directors has played a pivotal role in Wellspring's development and success over the years. The Board's story begins in 1983 with Ann Light, Wellspring's first Chairperson and greatest benefactor. An accomplished horsewoman and gardener, Ann grew up on a farm in Alabama, the daughter of a doctor. She adored her father and told stories of how he would never refuse services to anyone, but would accept chickens, eggs, and whatever else as payment. Oxford educated, Ann had a great love of literature and the arts, but remained always an immensely practical woman, who spoke her mind and was honest to a fault, saying it "like it is," no frills attached. Through her own woundedness, she was passionately supportive of mental health, which drew her to Wellspring.

Ann came to us through the Abbey of Regina Laudis, where she had been a major benefactor, providing funds for farm equipment for the nuns to use in cultivating and managing their land. The question for us was would our ardor and simple beginnings prove worthy of her support? Ann became devoted to the work of Wellspring. As "resident grandmother," she participated daily in group therapy, witnessing expressive work, dealing with caring confrontations, comforting a sobbing resident in grief work while someone else pursued their agenda. Although Ann found the raw emotional expression agonizing, she would never miss a group. On holidays, she would take residents into her home when they had nowhere else to go. As Wellspring faced seemingly insurmountable obstacles in the early days of this foundation, Ann would say, "As a horsewoman I learned that if you throw your heart over the fence first, the horse will follow."

After obtaining licensure as an Intermediate Treatment Facility, our next challenge – and Phyllis's crowning achievement as CEO – was to obtain the coveted accreditation from the

Joint Commission on the Accreditation of Hospitals (JCAHO). Although Wellspring originated outside of the mental health establishment, it became important to define ourselves professionally in relation to it if we were to survive and grow. Phyllis submitted to this detailed and demanding accreditation process, with the carrot of insurance coverage motivating her pursuit. Ann Light stepped forward as a "guardian angel" to finance a consultant for the JCAHO process, Winnie Downes. Working with fierce determination under Winnie's guidance, Phyllis addressed and implemented the 500-plus standards we were required to meet. Due to these efforts, we achieved JCAHO accreditation in 1984 as the smallest so-accredited behavioral health facility in the world. We have maintained this accreditation ever since, often with special commendation.

With the JCAHO accreditation in hand, facility expansion awaited us. Previously, Frank Rosseter, Wellspring's maintenance man for many years, had converted the large barn on the property to what is now the entry section of the Administration Building. Under Phyllis's leadership, and with Ann Light's generous financial support, we added to the Main House, built the Rosseter Barn (now the main building at the Arch Bridge School), and purchased both the Shiloah and Angelus Houses. This established the foundation and physical scope for what Wellspring was to be and become over the following decades.

To accompany this physical expansion, a Certificate of Need from the State of Connecticut was required to increase our licensed bed capacity. To accomplish this, Phyllis hired Herb Hall, formerly of The Country Place, to work with Bill Genovese, our Administrator at the time. They completed the Certificate during the winter and spring of 1986-87, working (and shivering) in a construction trailer parked on the front lawn beneath the hemlocks lining the driveway.

During this time, mental health insurance transitioned to a "managed care" model, and residential treatment at least initially was seen as a cost-effective alternative to extended hospital stays. Wellspring flourished for a time with the rapid influx of insurance-paid referrals, and we developed a working relationship with Four Winds Hospital in Katonah, New York, which became a major source of adolescent and young adult referrals.

1994 TO 1999

By the time Phyllis left the CEO role in 1994, the managed care boom was beginning to wane. Fortunately, this coincided with Herb Hall's retirement from employment with the State of Connecticut, and he stepped in to take over as Wellspring's second CEO. During the Certificate of Need process, Ann Light had been impressed with Herb and had invited him to stay on. He later said, "Ann paid me a compliment in the form of an offer I could not refuse." After first refusing the offer he couldn't refuse, in order to complete the requirements for his State pension, Herb honored Ann's "compliment" by becoming Wellspring's CEO.

Herb was a professional manager, just what we needed at the time to find our way through shrinking insurance coverage and shortened lengths of stay. From his earlier contact, Herb had responded deeply to the spirit of Wellspring. "I experienced Wellspring as a reviving, healing environment," he said, "and though I did not stay that long at first, I became inwardly committed to its mission." Herb had grown up on a farm in Western Pennsylvania and knew the healing power of hard work on the land. He also loved sailing, and perhaps his greatest gift to Wellspring was his steadiness at the tiller, as we worked our way through the challenges that faced us.

Many structural decisions had to be made. We shifted Angelus House from a halfway house to a residential treatment program for adults. Hugo Marchevsky and Gayle Pantaleo, a married couple of Wellspring team leaders, took over there as program directors. Dr. Earl Patterson, a former colleague of Herb's, became the Angelus psychiatrist for many years. The main campus then focused entirely on adolescent treatment, with residents housed in separate male and female programs. With the steady influx of adolescent referrals, the school shifted from a tutoring program housed in the basement of the Administration Building, to a full-time academic program with permanent classrooms in the Rosseter Barn.

Herb also had a gift for construction, and under his watch the maintenance shop on the first floor of the Rosseter Barn was moved to a new building of its own, where it has remained ever since. The animals were also moved from stalls in the barn basement and put out to pasture with minimal housing. This would change in 2007 with the construction of the Chapel Barn. During Herb's second term as CEO starting in 2002, the Administration Building was expanded to provide office space for administrators and therapists, a conference room, an art studio, and additional school classrooms.

Herb's management experience with state mental health was another of his assets. He knew many key people and was highly regarded for the programs he had run. With our increased reliance on adolescent referrals and shrinking insurance coverage, a positive relationship with the Department of Children and Families (DCF) was crucial. As a familiar and trusted manager, Herb provided a valuable interface with DCF in activating and negotiating publicly funded referrals. He was always cautious, however, about dependence on public funding, because he knew well how shifts in public policy, however well intended, were often out of touch with providers and could negatively affect both treatment and mission.

Herb's experience in the public sector was also instrumental in forging a relationship with the New York State Board of Education, a connection that has remained a major source of referrals to this day. As our reputation for quality treatment spread, self-pay admissions began to outstrip insurance as a source of revenue. Nevertheless, a balanced framework of revenue sources – insurance, DCF, school systems, and self-pay – remained the base of Wellspring's financial structure.

Following our licensing as an Intermediate Treatment Facility in 1981, we began to educate DCF and other agencies about the safety and healing power of our methods, and this continued under Herb. In response to the threat of shortened lengths of stay, and to avoid having treatment reduced to supportive containment, we were pressed to explore more intensive approaches. We concentrated our efforts on the treatment and parenting of traumatized, attachment resistant children, integrating this into our relational approach. We soon became known for this work through our residential and outpatient treatment. This led to requests for training in attachment therapy and parenting by DCF, Boys and Girls Village, and other regional agencies. This laid the groundwork for later presentations in Trauma Informed Care through the Wellspring Institute.

Herb's major achievement as CEO was the establishment of the Arch Bridge School, which was so named to distinguish it from Wellspring as a treatment agency. Under the leadership of Susan Schoenbach, Director of Education, the school had become a state approved Private Education Facility in 1997, able to admit day school students with special needs from surrounding districts. Faced with the surprising severity of emotional and behavioral problems in the day school population, Dan Murray, Director of the Adolescent Boys Program, was called upon to develop the school's clinical dimension. The use of Behavioral Specialists to supplement classroom teachers and a Relational Level System to help with behavioral management were the initial results of Dan's efforts. Parent involvement through bi-monthly Parent Support and Multi-Family Groups was soon mandated to deal with family related issues that affected education. These innovations were the beginnings of the Clinical Team at Arch Bridge and our Family Integration Model.

1999 TO 2002

When Herb asked to step down as CEO in 1999 to devote himself to the development of the school, the Board asked Richard – then Clinical Director – to step in and take Herb's place. He was by nature and education a therapist and clinician and was neither gifted nor trained for agency-level management. In response to the need, however, he reluctantly accepted the position. Hugo Marchevsky, who had replaced Bill Genovese as Chief of Operations, assured

Richard of his support, particularly with financial management. For the next three years, Richard filled in for Herb, while Herb worked to establish the Arch Bridge School on firmer footing.

Faced with a new and unfamiliar range of responsibilities, Richard stepped down as program director for the Adolescent Girls Program and appointed others in his stead. To maintain connection with residents and parents, however, he continued to conduct the Parent Support and Multi-Family Groups and the intake interviews for admission. This proved fortuitous. At the conclusion of a Parent Support Group in 1999, Tom Jasper approached Richard and asked him, "What do you do for fund raising?" Richard replied, "Next to nothing; we just work hard." Tom then agreed to come on the Board to help with our first concerted attempts at fund raising, and we hired a Director of Development to facilitate these efforts. Tom Jasper's recruitment initiated the development of Wellspring's Board of Directors from a collegial support group to a "working board."

With the help of Hugo Marchevsky, Wellspring's finances under Richard continued on solid footing, while walking our usual budgetary tightrope. We passed our triennial JCAHO inspection with commendation. On the other hand, the Adolescent Boys Program had been facing continual referral difficulties, and we made a decision to shift the program to the treatment of younger boys, age 7-12. Dan Murray, who remained at the program's head, developed the program into a wrap-around treatment model, with a residential step down to extended day treatment and therapeutic schooling, supported by Outpatient Services and Home Coaching.

With the development of the Arch Bridge School, Wellspring became an active presence in our surrounding communities. From its simple beginnings in 1997, nearly 80 different school districts in the State of Connecticut have referred students with special needs to Arch Bridge. The development of the school also spurred a corresponding development of Outpatient Services from support for residential clients in transition to a full-fledged community service. The initial thrust of Outpatient Services was in the attachment therapy and parenting for which we had become known, with a special focus on Home Coaching. The going was slow at first and didn't increase significantly until Mark Johnson was hired as Director of Outpatient Services in 2007 and we established the Wellspring Counseling Center.

2002 TO 2007

Richard ended his tenure as CEO in 2002, at which time Herb Hall returned for a second term at Wellspring's helm. Under Herb's leadership, Wellspring contracted with DCF to operate a

Group Home – which we called Pendana – on a separate property purchased on Judge Lane, just up the road. It was no surprise that DCF modeled their Group Homes after our family style children's residential program.

In 2004, Wellspring held a Board Strategic Planning Retreat which proved to be a watershed in our development. Part of the five-year strategic plan that emerged was a commitment by the Board to reinvigorate the land-based programs of work, animal care, gardening, and adventure. Although these programs were foundational to Wellspring's treatment philosophy, they had diminished over the years due to intensified clinical programming, building expansion, and the emergence of the Arch Bridge School. The Board also made a decision to explore the feasibility of a capital campaign to build a gym, an assembly space, and additional classrooms to fill out the school campus. Our fundraising consultants recommended that we test feasibility first by taking on a smaller project – the construction of a barn for the animals with a chapel. Michael Ackerman took the lead in fundraising for what became the "Chapel Barn Project," with the able assistance of Jim Churchill, a local contractor and former member of the Board. As a home for the animals and a meditation and prayer center for Wellspring as a whole, the Chapel Barn was finally completed in 2007.

Throughout this period, Wellspring began facing more difficult financial times. Insurance coverage had continued to diminish, and DCF referrals became more constricted with the development of the Group Home system as an alternative to residential. Only more seriously wounded children were being referred and many were unsuited to our relational form of treatment. While our younger children's program had been quite successful in terms of quality treatment, the lack of appropriate referrals was of increasing concern. Board development, on the other hand, had proceeded apace with an influx of several parents of former residents, who filled out the board profile with relevant professional skills. Requests for attachment-focused seminars and workshops for DCF and other agencies had continued to grow.

2007 TO 2011

When Herb announced his intention to retire in 2007, Wellspring was temporarily at a loss. It was clear to Herb and to Wellspring's Board that no one within the organization was prepared as yet for the job of CEO. A decision was made to search outside for someone with management experience, who might adapt to Wellspring's unique culture and further its mission. After numerous interviews with several executive managers, the Board chose Harvey Newman from New York City – a man with a background in social work with extensive experience as a CEO in the service of children.

Harvey was a godsend. From the start, he was attracted to Wellspring, though he had much to learn about its values, philosophy and relational approach. Evaluating staff and learning its organizational and financial structures was much simpler. Along with his superior leadership ability, Harvey was very intelligent and possessed a great capacity to listen, observe, experience and adapt. He also had a sharp eye for what was working and what was not. Harvey was a city man of Jewish heritage, sophisticated in many ways, but unused to working with land and animals. But he listened and learned from everyone, and especially from Dan Murray, his right-hand man as Clinical Director, who took the lead in Harvey's acculturation.

Harvey soon recognized Dan's capabilities, not only as a clinician and manager, but in budgeting and finance as well. Because of Harvey's respect and receptivity, Dan was able to collaborate on a number of important developments. He counseled and supported Harvey in trimming unnecessary staff and merging functions to help with the budget. He also worked with Harvey to discover a longstanding problem with State rate setting for Arch Bridge students and helped to correct this. Both moves helped Harvey deal with the nagging financial difficulties that continued to plague us throughout his five-year tenure. The main problem was chronic – the seasonal roller coaster of the school year, where census would drop sharply after June graduation, before building up gradually starting in September. Summer school and a Wellspring summer camp were efforts previously made to address this problem, and Harvey tried them again without greater success. The result was five years of minor but cumulative losses.

Harvey did have many significant achievements. Although Outpatient Services had started slowly under Mark Johnson in Middlebury, it soon flourished as a community counseling center with a vibrant intern training program. Sue Schoenbach, Director of Education at Arch Bridge, worked with Harvey to pursue New England Association of Schools and Colleges (NEASC) accreditation, the "gold standard" for schools in the Northeast. Harvey brought this process to its completion in 2011, with additional commendation by the National Association of Special Education Teachers (NASET) as a School of Excellence, an honor maintained for many years since.

Harvey was very personable with a delightful, wry sense of humor. He made a habit of regular visits to the school and each program to have lunch with students, residents and staff and to meet with the program directors. He got to know everyone through personal contact, and with his sharp eyes, assessed each program in the process. It was a way of management that had been impossible in the larger contexts of his former work. As a parallel to our "relational treatment," Harvey called this new management style "relational management," and wrote about it in articles he later published.

In retrospect, one of Harvey's greatest accomplishments was the development of Dan Murray as his successor. Under Herb, Dan had stepped into Richard's role as Clinical Director and had served in this role for more than a year when Harvey came on board. As Harvey became aware of Dan's gifts and sought his counsel, he in turn took on the mentoring of Dan as a CEO in preparation for his own retirement. When Harvey did announce his intention to retire in 2011, Dan was ready to take over the position with Harvey as his sponsor and the support of Richard and Phyllis.

2011 TO 2019

Dan's parents' strong work ethic and ability to overcome adversity helped shape his life and prepare him for the challenges of leadership. Dan's mother grew up quickly as one of eight children on a working farm without electricity or indoor plumbing and his father survived the tortures of a Nazi POW camp and came back home after the war to work two or three jobs throughout his life, while rising into a leadership role in a NY labor union. In fact, Dan's first Master's degree was in Organizational and Industrial Psychology, Psychology's answer to the MBA, and moving back toward the union was a potential early life plan. But healing and mental health care became passions for Dan and he went to work as a direct care staff in a private psychiatric hospital. During this time, he and his wife Laura were raising their young family and with Laura's support and encouragement, he worked toward his doctorate in Clinical Psychology. Dan's strong family values, background as an empowered direct care staff person and work experiences across several hospitals and clinics would serve him well across the programs and age groups at Wellspring.

Dan interviewed for a Psychotherapist position with Phyllis in 1991 and was struck by the beauty, depth and simplicity of Wellspring and its treatment model. He accepted the job quickly and by chance joined Richard's treatment team, one of three at the time, and began a 27+ year supervision relationship with Richard right away. At Wellspring, Dan has served as Psychotherapist, Team Leader, Clinical Supervisor, Program Director, and since 2006 as Chief of Professional Services & Clinical Director. His professional experience as both a manager and clinician, along with his early training in organizational psychology, coupled with 20+ years of supervision with Richard, equipped him fully for the CEO job.

The beginning of Dan's tenure soon led to a number of turning points. First, after several years of fiscal struggles, Wellspring began an extended period of prosperity, allowing more flexibility and less fear in future planning. Simultaneously in 2011, with Harvey and Dan's support and under the direction of Susan Schoenbach, Director of Education, Wellspring engaged in an accreditation process for the Arch Bridge School with the New England Association of Schools and Colleges (NEASC), the same organization that accredits Harvard and Yale. Wellspring's Arch Bridge School achieved this prestigious accreditation in 2012. With tearful eyes at the exit interview, the accreditation team told us how extraordinary we were at changing and saving lives and what a great educational experience we offered our students. Although their commendations were plentiful and resounding, they made a few recommendations, which we took to heart: You don't raise enough money, and you need a new building for the Lower School classrooms to replace the trailers, a cafeteria for day students, and a gym that also can be used for special events.

Dan responded to these recommendations by hiring a development professional and with the full support of the Management Team, staff and the Board, went about planning for the construction of a new centering building for the main campus. Wellspring then took a leap of faith and risked the launch of its first major Capital Campaign and redirected all of its development income into a campaign to raise $1.2 million. Phyllis stepped forward to assume leadership of the campaign and Wellspring raised upwards of a million dollars thanks to Board members, Wellspring parent alumni, friends, staff, and especially Isabella Dodds (for whom the Dodds Center is named) and her dear friend, Babette Basil. Three years later, Wellspring opened the Dodds Family Center for Arts and Athletics just as the school year began in September 2015. Wellspring's existing buildings and grounds also received a much-needed revitalization, both during and after the Dodds building process, with a complete overhaul of septic systems, roofs, kitchens, and much more. Dan's philosophy has always been to treat the programs, buildings and grounds like your own children or family members will be here and he joined with the Management Team and support staff to assure the warmth and quality of the buildings and grounds remained a priority.

Another major turning point during Dan's tenure came during early conversations with Isabella Dodds and Babette Basil, when they were first introduced to Wellspring by long time board member and dear friend Michael Ackerman. During these conversations, Wellspring's need for an Endowment to work toward assuring Wellspring's future started to take shape, as Babette Basil began to work with Isabella Dodds and her family's foundation to also make a signature gift to launch a Wellspring Endowment Fund. With Phyllis settled into a leadership role and partnering with the Wellspring Board of Directors for fund raising, Wellspring pivoted its efforts from building and furnishing the Dodds Family Center, to breathing life into Endowments to assure Wellspring's work for the future.

Wellspring has suffered a number of challenges in recent years, including the losses of our beloved co-founder, Richard Beauvais and our great friend and long-time Vice Chairman of the Board, Michael Berkowitz. These special men will be sorely missed by so many and for so many reasons. While their unexpected losses were heartbreaking, their spirits and generosity will live on at Wellspring, supported by the creation of the Richard & Phyllis Beauvais Endowment and the Michael Berkowitz Endowment for Angelus.

As Wellspring heads toward 2020, those we serve continue to get well and move back to their homes and schools with renewed health and academic success at extremely high rates. Thankfully, Wellspring's success remains tied tightly to our mission and values based in care and service, giving us a compass to always find our way forward in the future.

THE PATH FORWARD

In January 2019, Wellspring crossed a watershed, with Richard's unexpected death. At Richard's funeral, CEO Dan Murray offered the following words:

> AFTER CO-FOUNDING WELLSPRING WITH PHYLLIS IN 1977, RICHARD SPENT THE NEXT 40-PLUS YEARS OF HIS LIFE POURING HIMSELF INTO THIS SPECIAL PLACE AND BEING WITH EACH PERSON HE CAME IN CONTACT WITH, IN A PERSONAL WAY – AS CO-FOUNDER, THERAPIST, CLINICAL DIRECTOR, SUPERVISOR, TRAINER, CEO, BOARD MEMBER, CHAIRMAN OF THE BOARD, MENTOR, FRIEND…. RICHARD WAS A FORCE OF NATURE, LIKE A PASSIONATE WIND. HIS STRENGTH, UNDERSTANDING, AND CONVICTION SAVED AND CHANGED THE COURSE OF SO MANY LIVES. WHEN THE WINDS WERE CALM, HIS PASSION WAS NO LESS POWERFUL. HE COULD MELT HEARTS AND TOUCH SOULS. IN HIS 80TH YEAR OF LIFE, HE WAS STILL A VITAL PART OF WELLSPRING. HE WAS OUR CHAIRMAN OF THE BOARD, TRAINER, WRITER, MENTOR, AND ALWAYS FRIEND….
>
> TO BORROW A QUOTE FROM A NOTE PHYLLIS SHARED FROM ONE OF OUR WONDERFUL STAFF MEMBERS…RICHARD'S SPIRIT IS SO IMBUED IN WELLSPRING AND THAT IS SOMETHING I CONTINUE TO FEEL. HE IS A PART OF EVERY ADMISSION, EVERY FIRE BUILT IN THE FIREPLACE, EVERY CHOP OF WOOD, EVERY INTIMATE INDIVIDUAL SESSION, EVERY MEAL SHARED, EVERY TRIP TO THE ANIMALS… THE POET TAGORE WROTE: "I SLEPT AND DREAMT THAT LIFE WAS JOY. I AWOKE AND SAW THAT LIFE WAS SERVICE. I ACTED, AND BEHOLD, SERVICE WAS JOY."

Richard will be missed. But of course Wellspring's mission of service will continue to grow and deepen as we move into the decades to come. It is our hope that those who carry Wellspring forward will continued to be guided and nourished by the values and hard-won learning reflected in these pages.

CHAPTER 3

WELLSPRING'S PERSON-CENTERED, RELATIONAL APPROACH

A Friend is someone who remembers your beauty when you feel ugly; your wholeness when you feel broken; your innocence when you feel gullt; and your purpose when you are confused.

As set forth in Chapter 1, Wellspring's philosophy of healing is based on four core values; our approach is *personal, relational, intensive, and comprehensive*. In this chapter, we focus in particular on how our treatment philosophy embodies the first two of these values. We discuss what we mean by the "person," and how we work to *recover the person* through treatment. We describe the *therapeutic use of personality* in the client-staff relationship, our focus on *therapeutic parenting* in that relationship, and how all of this is incorporated into the broader *therapeutic community*. Finally, we discuss the central importance of safe, healing touch.

RECOVERING THE PERSON IN TREATMENT

At Wellspring, we base our approach to healing – and our entire therapeutic model – on a multi-dimensional concept of the *person*. "Person-centered recovery" is a commonly used term of art in mental health – referring to a collaborative approach to recovery from a mental health condition in which the patient as person plays a central and proactive role. At Wellspring, this approach could well be reframed as *recovering the person*, which we view as the ultimate goal of treatment.

In treatment, an individual is given a psychiatric diagnosis and is objectified as a particular disorder. But while useful for clinical practice, a diagnosis with its symptom cluster easily becomes a label, defining the individual as an "it" or object, rather than a "thou" or subject *(Martin Buber, I and Thou, 1958)*. Indeed, many clinical summaries are devoid of any sense of the person in terms of the essential nature and giftedness of the individual.

The cornerstone of Wellspring's relational approach is that inherent in each individual is a *wellspring* of personal being that is unique, unrepeatable and imbued with spirit. Our respect for the sacredness and dignity of each client proceeds from this belief. Fundamental to our relational approach, *personal being* is understood as a particular expression of all *Being*, which implicitly connects us with one another and all creatures. We emphasize this as a core treatment value, because there are forces within our culture and society that would erode this awareness.

At Wellspring, the work of *person recovery* has two complementary thrusts. One is to change unhealthy patterns of relationship to self and others that distort or block *who this person in essence actually is*. The second is to see and affirm this *personal* core, so that the individual can align with it and build upon it as the basis for a truly *personal* identity.

Our multi-modal and holistic treatment programs – which we discuss in greater detail in Chapters 4, 5, and 6 – provide different windows for seeing, mirroring, affirming and supporting the emergence of the *person* in the context of clinical work. Because *persons* are many-faceted and differently gifted, no single treatment modality or approach can serve all, but each contributes to the work of *person recovery* in its own particular way.

What staff bring to the process of *person recovery* is an alertness and receptivity to individual differences and the uniqueness of individual gifts. Because individuals cannot see their own nature, they take for granted what they do naturally and how they do it. What they need is to be seen, acknowledged and affirmed within an interpersonal framework focused on *person recovery*, so that they can begin to actively align with this deeper sense of who they are.

Personhood emerges only in the context of relationship; the two are inseparably linked. Individual therapy provides face-to-face intimacy and exchange, which is amplified in turn by relationships with staff in the milieu. Interactive group therapies provide a context for the individual to be seen as a *person* among peers, exploring individual differences and commonality with others through interpersonal engagement. Family therapy can work through problems in primary relationships that open to *person recovery* for both child and parents. A client may have been oppressed by her parents' vision of who she should be, or she may have been unseen altogether. In the process of treatment, parents recognize the re-emergence of the essential nature of their child, whom they had lost sight of but had known before.

Expressive Work is another important context for *person recovery*. By working through blocked emotions of anger, sadness, grief and joy, the individual can stand clear of defenses and be more vulnerable and real. With creative-expressive modalities and opportunities that encourage self-expression – art, music, drama, dance, puppetry, and sandtray, etc. – the creative product stands as a signpost of the *personal*.

At Wellspring, we maintain the presence and care of animals in all of our residential programs, because relationship with an animal simply makes us more human. It is why the non-verbal, land-based, experiential therapies of work, animal care, horticulture, and adventure program receive special emphasis, because nowhere is the essential nature of an individual more clearly revealed than in the instinctual response of body activity.

The same *personal* approach holds true in education, where learning disabilities and learning styles are approached individually. This is truly the art and the heart of "special education." Finally, the disorder itself can provide a window for *person recovery*. Symptoms can be understood as substitute ways to meet unmet needs – for attention, affection, appreciation, acceptance. But the *personal* can also be expressed through the symptom, whether in the artfulness of a defense or the style of a manipulation, the ways in which an individual strives to be special or to survive.

In these various ways, and to the degree that we as a therapeutic community direct our efforts toward *person recovery*, we provide an environment where treatment, education and healing are greatly enhanced.

THE THERAPEUTIC USE OF PERSONALITY

At Wellspring, the staff-client relationship – whether between the patient and the clinician, coverage staff or both – is critically important to our person-centered approach to the healing of emotional disorder. The apparent simplicity of this statement, however, belies its complexity – which rests on the consciousness and professional responsibility required to live it.

There are different types and levels of relationship, but for a relationship to be healing, it must be *personal*. The question is how can a relationship be truly personal when it is lived within the parameters set by professional responsibility for patient-therapist interaction? The *therapeutic use of personality* is an approach that can help resolve this paradox, but it requires some explanation.

We begin with the concepts of "transference" and "countertransference" – terms that psychologists use to describe unconscious projections onto another person of needs, feelings, fantasies, or beliefs rooted in some primary relationship (such as with a mother or father). So, for example, a patient may transfer feelings associated with the hated or loved father or mother onto a teacher, therapist, or coverage staff – causing the old relationship to be re-experienced and reacted to anew. Or a patient may attempt to obtain what was lacking in a primary relationship by finding the "good mother" or "good father" in someone perceived to possess those desirable qualities. Because projection by one person in a relationship invites counter-projection by the other, countertransference is to some degree the inevitable response to transference.

In a therapeutic relationship, the use of personality runs counter to traditional psychoanalytic practice, where the clinician intentionally limits personal exposure, so the transference can remain uncontaminated for analysis. At Wellspring, clinicians and coverage staff are actively involved in the residential milieu – eating, working and playing together – with their personalities continually exposed to client scrutiny. Instead of limiting personal exposure in the staff-client relationship, the challenge is how to channel this in ways that will make it more, rather than less, therapeutic.

By its very nature, the therapeutic relationship is skewed and one-sided in this respect, because inclusiveness and reciprocity cannot and should not be fully shared. While the client's life is being progressively opened, aspects of the staff person's life are necessarily left out of the equation. Given the nature and intent of the interpersonal exchange, a degree of mutuality can be achieved, but it remains "a mutuality forbidden to be full." Our focus here is on the degree and quality of mutuality that can be achieved in the staff-client relationship – what is included, as well as what is excluded.

At Wellspring, a primary task for clinical and coverage staff is to *see* and mirror *back* to the client the essential nature and giftedness of her being. This requires staff to look beneath the behavioral surface, as pathological and problematic as that may look, to *see* the core self of the other. Staff who see the essential *person* beneath the disorder are then more able to support the client in the healing process with "unconditional positive regard" (Rogers, 1953). For some clients, it is a way of being *seen* and *known* that they may never have experienced before. This ability to see the *person* beneath the pathology is not a result of technical knowledge, per se, but stems from an awareness of one's own person. When client care and clinical interventions proceed from this awareness, the relationship between staff and client can become healing.

To see the essential nature of an individual in this way often evokes in the staff person a response of both love and respect, whether or not the client is able to love herself. As one staff person said, "I will keep on caring for you until you are able to love yourself." To the degree that the staff person is able to establish and maintain this awareness, the client is related to as a *person* apart from a clinical delineation of symptoms and diagnosis. The relational ground for change is established in an essentially *personal* way.

A second challenge for staff is to be *present* to the client authentically as oneself. This means *being real* and *being with* the client in a way that is honestly engaged and authentic in self-expression and exchange. To do this, the staff person has to "overcome the tyranny of professional role," which can leave her encased and armored against personal exchange (Pilette, 1983). This establishes the other side of the "I-Thou" equation by revealing the staff *person* to the client through her authentic way of *being herself* and *being in relationship*, rather than through sharing information about her life.

The staff person's ability to risk relationship and remain honestly engaged also depends on the interpersonal skills she has at her command, because these skills must be exercised continually to meet the relational challenges the client presents – challenges which often intensify as a relationship develops. The authentic expression of feeling, for example, depends on the staff person's ability to be aware of and to regulate her own emotions, so that expression is not falsified but is calibrated to the needs of the client. The skills of *caring confrontation, caring feedback, intentional dialogue* (Hendrix, 1977), and *conflict resolution* are taught at Wellspring, and the exercise of these skills is not only fundamental to any successful relationship, but is a prime necessity for healing past relational wounds.

Human relationship is complicated because it confronts us with the genuine "otherness" of each individual. In this sense, relationship must become *conscious* – able to discern what belongs to me and what belongs to the other in any interaction. Jung's concepts of *Eros* and *Logos* are helpful in this regard. While *Eros* is the quality that connects us to others through feeling, empathy and compassion, *Logos* involves standing apart in order to reflect on what has transpired. Both capacities are necessary to relate with a client in a way that is both personal and therapeutic.

For staff, it is necessary to detach oneself from immersion in the relationship – *keeping one foot in and one foot outside of it* – for reflection and discernment. This attitude of *mindfulness* involves the ability to step back from the relationship and observe oneself in what has transpired. It involves an ongoing balancing act – engaging with the client through attunement, while remaining alert to manipulative "games" and transference/countertransference phenomena. Continual self-reflection about what is *of me* and what is coming *at me* is a difficult relational path to walk, which often requires the help of peer feedback and ongoing supervision. But these are issues that characterize the therapeutic relationship particularly, and to deal with them is neither a simple task nor is it ever complete.

What limits full mutuality in staff-client relationships is the degree of self-disclosure, for staff must be circumspect about what to share from their lives. The guiding principle is always *the good of the client*, and this must be determined by professional awareness and responsibility. The question to ask is *whose needs does sharing this information meet*, the client's or one's own. This can be confusing, because shared life experience can exercise an important teaching function in a therapeutic relationship. At the same time, the need of the client to feel special and privileged by more intimate disclosures may be what impels her curiosity and interest. When the staff person's narcissistic needs coincide with the client's interest, the impulse to self-disclosure can lead to inappropriate sharing, which inadvertently invites the client into a sense of responsibility for the staff person that can be burdensome.

Instead of being without boundaries, the use of therapeutic personality in relationship maintains boundaries that are subtle and flexible, rather than rigid. Self-disclosure is open in some ways, particularly in the authentic expression of feeling and the directness of interpersonal communication, but it is limited in sharing information from one's private life.

Informal social contact is similarly circumscribed, limited to contact in the residential setting or on scheduled outings.

A similar boundary applies to social contact outside of the residential program after treatment has ended. Return visits by a resident are encouraged, but require permission. Staff should be informed of visits in advance, if only to assure that the former resident will be properly received. The *personal* bond developed while in residence requires protection in the face of subsequent relationships developed with other residents, which can activate jealousy or perceived rejection by the visitor.

When a relationship with a resident has been established, it is important that no artificial cutoff be imposed. Being cared for and becoming competent are not mutually exclusive and should not be made so. Our work is to help the client resolve the *rapprochement dilemma* of early childhood, and to become independent and competent without losing love. Continued contact by phone or letter should not be discouraged, but should be regulated with the good of the client as the overriding concern.

To the degree that a client develops in personhood and is able to discern and take responsibility, relating to the clinician or coverage staff without illusion or projection, a former staff-client relationship can evolve over time into a more fully human relationship based on true friendship and mutual regard.

THERAPEUTIC PARENTING

The relationship between staff (therapist, nurse, milieu counselor, teacher, etc.) and client has different aspects: professional, parent, teacher, mentor, friend. Whatever form or forms this takes, we consider this relationship to be an integral part of the healing process. As we explain below, at Wellspring we place particular importance on the *parenting* dimension of the staff-client relationship.

Because pathology is usually organized around relational wounds, the healing process in some way must consist of repeated *corrective emotional-relational experiences*. Whether these wounds come from rejection, abandonment, neglect, or suppression of emotional expression, there is some degree of developmental injury that impairs parent-child bonding and attachment, which affects the capacity for healthy independence.

The original trauma may have been physical or emotional, but it is always experienced as relational. For individuals whose pathology is organized around early developmental issues, analysis can be useful, but is not in itself emotionally or physically powerful enough to provide the needed transformative emotional- relational experience. If a baby was unloved and unnurtured, it is not enough simply to know that. Some actual experience of being loved and nurtured is needed for healing to occur. Similarly, if the young child was not given behavioral limits, was allowed to tyrannize others and consequently suffered rejection, it is not enough for her to know that. She must have actual experience of the corrective alternative within the context of trusted relationships, in order to incorporate the value of limit setting for socialization.

Intensity and continuity of interpersonal relationship within residential treatment can provide both the awareness and transformative experience necessary for healing. Because the first experience of bonding occurred within the mother-child relationship, Wellspring approaches healing this wound within the context of *therapeutic parenting*. Healing comes through cognitive understanding and new experiences of the "inner child" in relationship with a skilled and caring parenting person. To talk about "trust" or "bonding" or "healthy child" may be useless for an individual who has had little or no experience of trust, bonding, or a healthy childhood. This experience is first sensory-physical, then emotional, and then cognitive, but it is always relational, contained within the crucible of the "parenting" relationship.

We know that the traumatic experiences of childhood are dramatic and powerful in their impact, and they may require equally dramatic and powerful relational experiences as the media for healing. Because we contain all of our developmental history within us, and because the original drama affected us as children, the healing drama must also meet and affect the experiential underpinnings of this "inner child." The structures we have developed for *therapeutic parenting* are designed to provide these alternatives. The task, however, is not to regress to childhood or to remain a child, but to internalize a healthy parent ego state and develop a clear and competent adult ego state, in order to free the "inner child" from the bondage of pathology. In effect, this learning is ultimately about how to parent oneself.

When we speak of *therapeutic parenting*, we are in no illusion that we are taking the place of the original parents, nor do we wish to do so. In fact, our effort is to invite and educate the parents to become more effective, particularly when discharge involves the resident's return home. Our basic assumption in this regard is that parents have done the best they can with what they know. But their parenting style is often passed down from their own parents, or they have rejected their parenting without an effective alternative. The general shift from an authoritative to a permissive style of parenting is a case in point. Family therapy and the therapeutic milieu are contexts where problems with parenting are revealed and addressed. Parent Support Group and Multi-Family Group in our Adolescent, Girls, and Day School Programs are additional contexts where parent training can occur.

Therapeutic parenting is more difficult than normal parenting, and requires more sophisticated training, although it is based on the same principles. It is more difficult because it has the task of addressing already established problematic patterns of relationship and defense which were formed in response to early childhood circumstances and events. *Therapeutic parenting* demands both an understanding of how to meet psychopathology with care and the skill to re-educate the client in healthy patterns of relationship.

Sometimes failure in bonding occurs because parents lack the skills of normal parenting, but in many cases parents who would be successful in normal circumstances are faced with a child who has suffered physical or emotional trauma and whose healing requires special skills. This may require an entire system of supportive relationships, and the parents usually are not able to provide that level of care or treatment. Those whose physical or emotional trauma occurred later in life, for whom there was already a successful completion of bonding as well as some degree of separation/individuation, may not need this level of intervention.

It is beyond our scope here to discuss child development or elucidate methods of healthy parenting. We have found the materials on parenting and corrective parenting available within the Transactional Analysis literature to be particularly useful in this regard. We have also found the writings of D.W. Winnicott within the psychoanalytic literature to be instructive in terms of providing "primary experience" to fill in early developmental gaps. The materials on pre- and perinatal trauma within the emotional expressive literature are also useful, particularly with the adaptations developed within our own Emotional Expressive Therapy.

We think that the practice of *therapeutic parenting* proceeds from the following principles and is based on the following skills and abilities:

1. The ability to see, love and mirror the essential nature of the client *unconditionally*. This capacity for unconditional love must involve the parenting person's whole being – body, heart, mind and spirit.

2. This unconditional "love" does not mean discounting or ignoring obnoxious or pathological behavior, but it does mean "seeing through" the behavior to the essential nature and emotional needs of the child within.

3. It is important to accept the individual *as she is*, but this does not mean wanting her to stay as she is. It means being willing to accept where she is at this point in time, including her pathology – and a willingness to work patiently as she develops the understanding, experience, and the strength to make healthier choices.

4. Skill is needed to structure therapeutic experiences that will mirror, affirm and meet the needs of the "inner child" and to contract with the client and family to explore these experiences, whether through school, work, play, healthy touch, creative-expressive media, or activities of daily living.

5. Competence is needed to provide cognitive information and to foster dialogue related to these therapeutic experiences, in order to reflect and think about them together with the client both before and after they occur.

6. Sophistication is needed to differentiate between times when it is developmentally appropriate to gratify needs, or help the client to delay gratification, or to develop alternative means of gratification, or simply to analyze these needs in order to better understand them. This requires an understanding of *symbiosis* (enmeshed dependency) and how to resolve it.

7. The ability to confront pathology or maladaptive behavior and demand appropriate alternatives, while maintaining the stability afforded by unconditional love, within an attitude of care and respect.

8. An artful sense of timing, knowing/sensing how much "truth" the client is able to face or bear at this particular moment and to calibrate treatment interventions in manageable doses.

9. The willingness to bear the pain of negative or positive transference and to share this process with peers and supervisors collaboratively within the therapeutic community.

10. Willingness to risk mistakes and then to admit, apologize and rectify them, both as an honest commitment to truth and as a way of modeling for the resident.

11. Awareness of one's own feelings and needs and a willingness to speak them truthfully within the relationship, while maintaining professional boundaries and a sensitivity to the feelings and needs of the client.

12. A sense of humor and playful creativity with the ability to free this capacity in others.

13. An ability to impart healthy values and provide clear parenting messages appropriate for each developmental stage.

14. An ability to think clearly and to teach problem solving.

15. An ability to commit oneself to the becoming of the person, and to support the continuity of that becoming.

16. The willingness to risk friendship – that is, to allow the client to resolve transference issues, grow up, and move from a relationship of therapeutic dependence to independence and potential friendship. "Success" in treatment should not lead to loss of relationship.

THERAPEUTIC COMMUNITY AS A HEALING THEATER FOR THE SELF

At Wellspring, the relationship between staff and clients is situated within – and benefits from – the broader *therapeutic community*. One of the advantages a therapeutic community offers over private practice is that the variety of players can assume multiple transferential roles. Using the metaphor of *theater*, we might say that each resident who comes to Wellspring brings with her a psychological drama that is partly conscious, but mostly unconscious. Insofar as the psyche of the resident has been wounded, fragmented, she will, within the residential "theater" of Wellspring, begin to "cast" or transfer the fragmented parts of herself onto various members of the community. One may be cast as the "rejecting mother," another as the "nurturing mother," another still as the "absent father," and another as the "ideal father."

At the point where the community begins to experience these transferential "splits," there is a fertile moment where the staff can, through communication and shared consciousness, bring these fragments together and help the client "rewrite" the script of pathology into a drama of healing.

This depends on bringing the major "players" together in the same room to communicate with one another first, and then to communicate with the resident about the various sub-personalities cast throughout the community, as a way to increase consciousness for all. To have all of the key players on the same page, not to change their roles as such, but to work together for the good of the resident, provides the "flip" which can reframe the drama from a negative and pathological one to one that is positive and healing. The possibility of making use of this very powerful intervention is dependent upon the willingness of staff from the various modalities to communicate with one another and come together in a collaborative approach. It also requires staff who are "caught in the split" to be willing to call in a "director" from within the community – someone who stands "outside of the drama" – to help choreograph the "split parts" into a new and healing whole.

THE IMPORTANCE OF SAFE, HEALING TOUCH IN TREATMENT

Throughout our history, Wellspring has used *safe, healing touch* as a dimension of treatment. Taking the form of a gentle hug, backrub, or supportive hand, it is most often used in the context of group or family therapy and is always done pursuant to Wellspring's approved protocols and staff training. Never sexualized or aggressive, touch at Wellspring is supportive, comforting and nurturing.

Safe, healing touch is presented and discussed with residents and their parents and is always based on their permission. In addition to its use in group or family therapy, our residents may ask for hugs or supportive touch from trained staff in common areas at Wellspring at times when they feel upset and need comfort. It is a powerful tool in preventing the escalation of emotional dysregulation. Parents are also invited and encouraged to learn our approach with their children.

Safe, healing touch is profoundly soothing and profoundly relational. Operating at a sensory-emotional level of communication, touch is an especially meaningful component in the treatment of cumulative trauma and attachment difficulties. Focused on healing the wounds of early trauma and inadequate attachment, it helps fill in developmental gaps in relational support and nurturing. Because pain and fear accrue from unmet needs, children have often disconnected from their inherent attachment system, through which they evoke and depend on the care of adults. Trust in adults fails to develop along with a sense of self as worthy and deserving of care. Building trust and a sense of self-worth and confidence in being able to ask for and receive needed comfort is a critical factor in the healing of relational trauma.

Safe, healing touch is ideally suited to address these problems. Clinical results and client feedback have consistently affirmed the positive effects of these interventions with children, adolescents, adults, and families.

CONCLUSION

Our focus on the person is at the heart of Wellspring. We begin with the fundamental dignity and uniqueness of each person – with the "recovery of the person" as our therapeutic north star. In pursuing this goal, we focus on personal relationship – the staff-client relationship and especially therapeutic parenting, the building of a therapeutic community, and the assurance of both healthy connection and safety through safe, healing touch. This is the touchstone for everything we do – every program, every house, and every treatment modality.

CHAPTER 4

INTENSIVE AND COMPREHENSIVE: WELLSPRING'S MODEL OF RESIDENTIAL TREATMENT

Inherent in each individual is a wellspring of personal being that is unique, unrepeatable and inbued with spirit.

We turn now to the third and fourth core values that animate Wellspring's approach to healing: that treatment be *intensive* and *comprehensive*. Wellspring's model is centered on residential treatment or residential treatment in a private school environment. Over the years, we developed our model of residential treatment to meet the challenges we confronted on the way, not the least of which has been an attack on residential treatment altogether. Although the need for this intensive form of treatment remains critical, particularly in the comprehensive way we do it, the case for its efficacy must continually be made.

Our approach can be summed up in the following simple phrase: *Integrated treatment and education for long-term results*. Our goal is to support successful transitions from hospital to home and school or to independent living, and to provide a flexible continuum of care to support the transition process through step-down options and outpatient services. In support of that goal, we use an intensive and holistic model of care, which integrates multiple therapeutic modes with an accredited private school – including individual and family therapy, emotional expressive therapy, land-based experiences, and creative-expressive therapies. In this chapter, we delve further into the philosophy underpinning this approach – before turning, in Chapters 5 and 6, to discussion of Wellspring's residential programs and therapeutic modes as they exist today.

INTENSIVE RESIDENTIAL TREATMENT SUPPORTS TRANSITION

Wellspring's model of residential treatment allows for an intensive level of care we believe necessary to support real healing and long-term results. As discussed in the preceding chapter, this model allows for a greater depth of relationship engagement within the crucible provided by the therapeutic community. While our goal is the recovery of the person, our model has also always fundamentally been about transition – transition to home and school for adolescents and transition back to college or to independent living for young adults.

Because psychiatric hospitalization is a disruptive event for anyone, but especially for a child and family, the challenges for successful transition are complex and difficult. Hospital stays these days are very brief, and the adolescent or young adult has to cope with medication adjustments, restoring relationships, managing an awkward return to school or employment, and finding a way to resume meaningful interests and activities. No transition is ever seamless, no aftercare simple or easy.

If the individual suffers from depression and has resorted to the harmful coping skills of drug abuse and self-harm that often accompany it, recovery becomes even more complicated and volatile. Family relationships are often strained or explosive, and the need for re-hospitalization is ever-present. Younger children may continue to be out of control, unable to be safely contained either at home or in school. These are complex problems, which outpatient treatment, however intensive, is often inadequate to address.

Families usually do not consider residential treatment as a viable option. While parents may desperately need respite, they also know they need more than a holding tank for their child; and regrettably a holding tank is all that many residential programs provide. Containment has its benefits, no doubt. It can relieve parents from having to forcibly restrain an out-of-control child and can save the adolescent or young adult, at least temporarily, from substance abuse, self-injury and suicide. But the containing situation has to offer more than respite. It must provide a container for healing that does *the real work of transition home*.

What is that "real" work? For adolescents and many young adults, family therapy is certainly its cornerstone, much as some parents might like to avoid this unpleasant truth. The myth that the child can be "fixed" outside of the family system while that system remains unchanged, was debunked long ago. Although the child may be the identified patient, the family system also needs work. Parents may have done the best they can with what they know, but often they practice what they've learned from their own parents, and family problems can be handed down through generations. Foster and adoptive parents may blame the child's biological parents before them, but successful engagement requires that they accept their own responsibility in the family dynamic.

If residential treatment is to provide a viable transition, the family needs to be actively involved. Family therapy must be regular and intensive if relationships are to be restored or, in many cases, newly developed. The capacity for honest emotional communication must be opened to restore or establish heart-to-heart connections. New parenting skills have to be learned and practiced in the therapeutic milieu and on visits home, as soon as it is safe for the child to venture home. These visits cannot be little vacations from treatment where parents and kids tiptoe around each other, not wanting to rock the boat. They have to extend the work begun in family therapy with clear tasks set out for both parents and child, not the least of which is to learn to have fun together. Both the successes and the glitches need to be processed after visits. Only when this work has been undertaken and parenting and communication skills have been developed and practiced, is the child ready to return home to parents prepared to receive her.

Substance abuse, self-harm and suicidality complicate any transition, and visits home must be closely monitored. Random drug testing may maintain sobriety within the residential setting, but slips on home visits can provide learning opportunities as well as indicators of whether and when a resident/client is ready for discharge. The adolescent or young adult and the parents must all be involved in psychoeducation about drugs and drug abuse. Alcoholics Anonymous meetings for substance abusers may be attended while in residence and on home visits, so that commitment to sobriety and an ongoing support system are in place prior to discharge.

Positive peer relationships are a crucial need of adolescents and young adults, who often use drugs and drinking as ways to belong. Adolescents and young adults in need of residential care often have poor social skills and lack the ability to form meaningful friendships. Interpersonal skill training is, therefore, an essential component of both residential treatment and the transition process. Clients need to learn how to assert themselves and ask for what they need, deal with limit setting and caring confrontation, and develop the capacity for honest dialogue and conflict resolution.

Everyone in residential treatment needs to learn *how to work on oneself*. Newer residents have often heard this phrase and can parrot it back, but they rarely have a clue about what it means. To be prepared for transition and aftercare, they need to develop healthy coping skills in place of negative ones. They need to experience therapy, not as something "done to them," but something that works for them and in them to improve their lives. Perhaps the most crucial dimension of therapy is the *emotional expressive work* needed to become aware of feelings and to learn how to express them appropriately in relationships. A positive experience of therapy in residential treatment can help an adolescent or young adult to become an active agent in outpatient treatment, which will depend entirely on what they bring to the table.

Because emotional disorder and behavioral problems interfere with concentration and study, academics suffer accordingly. Adolescents and young adults often have fallen behind or dropped out of school. Within the residential setting, supportive special needs education, discussed in greater detail below, has several tasks. Small classes provide for personal attention, support for different learning styles, and help in coping with learning disabilities. The appreciation of different learning styles and personal gifts are aspects of academic work that diminish shame and build self-confidence, making a successful return to mainstream education possible.

It goes without saying that good psychiatry and a competent nursing staff are critical elements of residential treatment that also support transition. Each of Wellspring's residential programs is supported by quality psychiatric care and 24-hour nursing coverage – as well as nutritional consultation and guidance. Unlike outpatient care, a supportive residential setting can test medications to see what's actually needed and what helps, in contrast to medication add-ons for symptom control. As the resident becomes healthier through treatment, medications may be either diminished or discontinued.

Successful transition best occurs in calibrated steps until the major building blocks are secure. While the residential experience differs from real life, because of its structure and level of supervision, life in some ways has been more real, because relationships have been built upon honest self-disclosure and exchange. Parents have had the opportunity to do their own work and are grateful for what they've learned, although all will say it hasn't been easy. Although transition from residential treatment presents many of the same problems as before, from this new vantage point they are experienced and encountered much differently.

AN INTEGRATED MODEL OF CARE

Wellspring's comprehensive and intensive approach to residential treatment in a quality private school environment has offered a compelling and much-needed alternative to unsuccessful, risky and even hurtful child welfare based residential program models. These child welfare models have been either (a) short-term or respite-type treatment models, originally created for adolescents with severe behavior problems that placed the dangers and burdens back on parents, families and local schools too quickly and risked family disruptions, or (b) their signature "warehouse" models that provided a long-term living situation for large groups of children. These historical long-term warehouse-type programs failed miserably and helped turn everyone against the concept of residential treatment. The warehouse model typically offered behavior modification along with recreational activities; socialization and family involvement were minimal. By necessity, educational programs were connected to them, but they usually had much lower expectations and were able to avoid teacher and school credentialing.

Wellspring instead provides an integrated family inclusion model of care that combines clinically intensive residential treatment with quality special needs education; the comprehensive use of different treatment modalities acting in concert; and a blend of transitional step-downs, with a therapeutically focused day school and outpatient services in a continuum of care.

At Wellspring, clinically intensive residential treatment is integrated with education in a way that is unique in the realm of therapeutic schooling. Each component is accredited by top-flight agencies – Wellspring by The Joint Commission (TJC) and its Arch Bridge School by the New England Association of Schools and Colleges (NEASC). The Arch Bridge School serves Wellspring's residential programs – girls, adolescents, and young adults – and also functions as a Therapeutic Day School for students bussed from surrounding districts. Since its accreditation by NEASC in 2012, the Arch Bridge School has been acclaimed regularly as a School of Excellence by the National Association of Special Education Teachers (NASET).

At the second level of integrated care – that of program – the approach to treatment and education is *personal* and *relational*. The *personal* dimension is based on a cultivated awareness and response by staff to the unique nature and giftedness of each resident or student. This involves a deeper look at the individual than diagnosing a disorder or a learning disability. It is a concerted effort to see, affirm and foster this *personal* core through staff and family relationships. Joined with clinical experience and skill, this approach gives depth to how emotional, behavioral and learning issues are addressed and helps stabilize the treatment and educational process.

This personal and relational approach is fully integrated into program design. Disorders and learning disabilities are complex, but so are people. Because each person responds differently, no single modality or approach can meet all the needs of a given individual. Program design must be comprehensive to address the different aspects of a disorder, but it must also be holistic to touch the mind, heart, body and spirit of a person.

Treatment is centered by individual, group, and family therapy. Milieu therapy in the school and residences supports this work with particular attention to peer and staff relationships. As parental relationships become transferred to milieu staff in their "parenting" roles, the acting out of these patterns is focused back into individual and family therapy. Multiple interactive group therapies concentrate on developing self-assertion, caring feedback, caring confrontation and conflict resolution. These skills in turn funnel back into family therapy, parent support, and multi-family groups to address problems and reconstitute family relationships. In these different ways, the interpersonal world of the resident becomes the practical school for relational development.

The integration of different modalities can have a synergistic effect on treatment, but this is accomplished only through close collaboration – no small matter to achieve. An essential part of the mix is Expressive Group, designed to evoke, express and process the blocked emotions of sadness, anger, fear and pain so basic to affective disorders and post-traumatic stress disorder. Primary therapists are present in these groups to integrate intense emotional expression in follow-up individual work. This becomes a bridge in turn to convert raw emotional expression into the appropriate communication of feelings in peer groups and family therapy.

Creative therapies– such as Art and Sandtray, discussed in greater detail in Chapter 6 – evoke and reflect a sense of self, a sense of "who I am." These creative media work in concert with the physical activities of Animal, Gardening, Work, and Adventure programs for the same end. The individuality expressed through creative media has its embodied counterpart in the instinctual responses revealed by the resident in hands-on work with staff and peers. These land-based media also build ego strength through learning how to work and by developing a work ethic to meet the challenges life will present.

Land-based programs – also discussed in Chapter 6 – are often thought of as a luxury, but at Wellspring they are considered essential. Richard Louv, in his book *The Last Child in the Woods*, coined the phrase "nature deficit disorder" to characterize the unhealthy effects of young people's increasing disconnection from nature through fixation on virtual reality. Camping, canoeing, ropes course, and the camaraderie of shared work and play experiences make involvement with nature inviting and help to correct this imbalance.

From a belief in the whole person, Wellspring is intentionally countercultural in this regard. Immersion into soil that grows vegetables and flowers is different than getting dirty, though in an adolescent's mind it may start out the same. Getting to know a chicken, a lamb, a goat, or a rabbit can be a revelation to an adolescent otherwise cut off from these experiences. So can camping out in the woods, or caving. Most adolescents have never engaged in community service – never helped in a soup kitchen or washed cars to raise money for a local ambulance service that serves them. They discover satisfaction in helping others, and in so doing discover themselves.

Which brings us to the third level of integration – the continuum of care available to residents, students and families as they progress in treatment. This continuum is multi-faceted and situational. As a resident-student progresses in the residential context, she may step down to less intensive treatment similar to a therapeutic school. If living locally, she may attend the Arch Bridge Day School while participating in residential groups and meeting with her primary therapist in individual and family work. Young adults may attend college classes while in residence, preparing for eventual return to full-time college. Or they can take a part-time job while in residence as preparation to live independently nearby. They can then be in partial care and spend two or three days a week at Wellspring, connecting with friends still in residence while continuing to see their primary therapist as an outpatient.

In other words, a care continuum is fashioned individually based on readiness and flexibly blended services to provide the necessary support. Residential step-down opportunities include day school, therapeutic schooling, part-time employment, outpatient therapy, and off campus living as available options. The intent, where possible, is to provide support through established relationships, because continuity of relationship is a crucial factor in managing transitions. While the goal is always to make transitions as seamless as possible, change is never seamless. It can, however, be made less bumpy and disjointed.

Wellspring's model of integrated care fosters personal integration with continuity of relationship to stabilize the process. Although the work is arduous and never-ending, we know from long experience the value and effectiveness of this approach for the residents, students, and families we serve.

CHAPTER 5

WELLSPRING'S RESIDENTIAL AND SCHOOL PROGRAMS

The wounds of emotional disorder were developed through relationships.

Therefore, relationship must be the primary medium for healing.

Throughout Wellspring's first four decades, there has been continuity in our fundamental values and our personal, relational, intensive, and comprehensive approach to treatment – as discussed in Chapters 1, 3, and 4, above. But as the overview of Wellspring's history in Chapter 2 makes clear, our specific programs – and the physical spaces that house them – have evolved over time, as needs and resources have shifted. We expect that will continue to be so, as Wellspring evolves and grows through the decades to come. Still, there is value in describing Wellspring's core programs as they exist today – and how each of these reflects the values and approach that have guided us from our founding, and which will continue to do so as we move forward.

At the time of this writing, Wellspring encompasses five programs: an Adolescent Girls Residential Program for girls ages 13-18 (located at Beauvais House, on our main campus); a younger Girls Residential Program for middle school girls (located at Shiloah House, on our main campus); an Adult Residential Program for adult women (located at Angelus House, on a separate campus); the Arch Bridge School, a private therapeutic special education school serving both residential and day students (located on our main campus); and Wellspring Counseling Services, an outpatient services program providing services for children, adolescents, and adults, with individual, group, and family treatment. In addition, the Wellspring Institute provides training, seminars, and workshops – at Wellspring, neighboring school districts, and beyond.

In this Chapter, we share insights from our three residential programs based on interviews with the managers of these programs – along with a brief overview of the Arch Bridge School adapted from an essay by the school's first director. In the case of the residential programs, we focus on how Wellspring's values and approach are expressed through the program's "milieu" – a term we use to refer to the overall social and therapeutic environment, including everyday interactions among residents and between residents and staff, as well as the integration of various other therapeutic approaches, such as creative-expressive or land-based programs. In the following Chapter, we will turn to a discussion of the various modalities of therapy Wellspring integrates in its overall approach. As the sketches below illustrate, each of Wellspring's programs is unique – but each expresses our core values and fundamental approach, founded on healing the uniquely gifted "person" through interpersonal relationship and healthy parenting.

ADOLESCENT GIRLS RESIDENTIAL TREATMENT PROGRAM-BEAUVAIS HOUSE

The residents who come to Wellspring's Adolescent Girls Residential Treatment Program typically present with issues that stem from, but are not limited to, mood disorders, personality disorders, eating disorders, attachment difficulties, anxiety disorders, post-traumatic stress disorder, and substance abuse in partial remission. Wellspring's relationally based approach, combined with a highly structured and highly nurturing home-like atmosphere, provides daily living experiences of relationship with staff and peers. This process promotes an emotionally and physically safe environment for healing. The Wellspring "family" experience becomes an essential part of family therapy, and family involvement in the treatment process is critical.

Each resident participates in a robust set of clinical offerings – including individual therapy, family therapy, multiple interactive group therapies, a Parent Support Group and Multi-Family Group, and Emotional Expressive Therapy Groups. Residents also participate in land- and body-based programs (Work, Animal Care, Gardening, Recreation and Adventure) as well as creative expressive therapy (Art Therapy and Sandtray), all of which are discussed in greater detail in the following chapter.

As in all of Wellspring's programs, there are two somewhat distinct but interconnected aspects of the Beauvais House milieu – the *interpersonal milieu* of relationship among residents and between residents and staff, and the *experiential milieu*, which includes Activities of Daily Living and recreation, along with the land-based programs. The milieu is meant to provide an interpersonal crucible where expectations are held and everything can be challenged. In the milieu, we make "mountains out of molehills" because the smallest thing is writ large in its implications for others. We emphasize awareness of how the behavior of each person affects others, which is different from what may feel okay for any given individual.

In Wellspring's relational model generally, and specifically in our approach in the milieu, we strive to hold both *nurture* and *structure*. In terms of structure, Activities of Daily Living are very important. These include basic responsibilities for self-care and room care, which are also ways of participating in community life, because in community everything one does or doesn't do impacts on others. Chores like setting tables, doing cleanup, taking care of your room, taking care of yourself, all bring order to one's personal life by ordering the environment. They also reflect disorder in the same way, and that affects the people with whom you live.

Nurture in the milieu occurs on many levels starting with the atmosphere of Beauvais House. The front room with its huge fireplace makes an ideal living room. The kitchen at the center of the house, with its wraparound windows integrating the pasture and hillside, is a "hearth," as all avenues run through it. Residents participate in cooking through a formal program – but there also are informal opportunities to engage, relax and "be" with staff and other residents around this centering space. Parents and residents alike are comforted by Beauvais House's homelike tenor and décor.

Therapists are actively involved with the milieu when they're on the "floor." They rotate meal coverage during the week. While one or two therapists eat with the kids, the others may also join in or be around, but everyone at the meal participates in cleanup – contributing and intermingling.

In the milieu, we strive to teach healthy relationship by modeling it – with a particular focus on parenting. Therapists and staff hold expectations, set limits, give support, comfort and nurturance, and teach social skills. Staff have to deal with a lot of parent transference and countertransference issues. They are challenged to become conscious of that dimension of relationship, particularly when holding structure, and how their unconscious feelings may be communicated non-verbally through body language.

We work to teach respect for parents and authority. We often find that parents have given their kids the message that "we're afraid of you and you're in charge," or "we don't think you're safe." At Wellspring, we help parents learn not to be afraid of their kids. Restoring respect for parental authority starts with helping parents to stop trying to be friends with their kids – and instead to take on the job of being parents. Our work in the milieu supports this endeavor; when parents see how kids respond to our expectations around self-care, honest engagement, and the environment, they often are amazed.

Each resident's primary therapist centers and coordinates the development of a treatment plan in an honest relationship with each resident and family, and our psychiatrist oversees and supports that. With so many different modalities, treatment planning is like weaving a tapestry. We have input from all of the different modalities about the social, emotional and functional levels of the girls, and we work to integrate all of that. That's an ongoing effort, because in the residential milieu of a therapeutic community you experience everything – how kids are differently gifted, what they respond to, and where and how they struggle with themselves, with each other, and with staff. The milieu provides the grounding for a process-oriented treatment in the midst of a clinically intensive program.

GIRLS RESIDENTIAL TREATMENT PROGRAM-SHILOAH HOUSE

Wellspring's Girls Residential Treatment Program at Shiloah House serves girls 11-15. Residents in this small, individualized program present with a variety of emotional problems and diagnoses including bipolar and mood disorders, post-traumatic stress disorder and anxiety disorders, ADHD, attachment difficulties, school phobia, and emerging personality disorders. This program is smaller and even more intimate than the adolescent program at Beauvais house. The program's therapists are present throughout the day and participate in daily activities alongside residents. Residents come home from school for lunch at Shiloah House at midday, taking part in the cooking and prep work beforehand. They then have an experiential group, such as yoga or gardening, before going back to school. In this and many other ways, the Shiloah milieu mixes "home" with school – nurture with structure, which is the basis of Wellspring's relational approach.

Nurture is fundamental, and we focus on affirming our kids in every way that we can. We make eye contact and request it from them. We're honest with them even when it's hard. We often catch them doing something right and say, "I like that you did that! Great teamwork!" And we give them evidence, so they know it's true and not just words: "I like that you're such a hard worker in the garden. When you're done with a task, you ask for another instead of waiting for me to notice that you're done. I love that about you." But perhaps the most basic way we nurture kids is through affirming and validating who they are beyond how they've been labeled. We look beyond the problematic behaviors to see and reflect back the basic goodness in them. And we regularly assure each kid that we care about who they are and where they're headed, which reinforces a source of identity in them and offers hope.

While we hold a structure, we try to be as relationally flexible as we can. When a kid with disordered eating doesn't want to eat, offering choices around food can avoid unnecessary power struggles. We always look for things they like to do that we can do with them. For instance, one resident loves car rides, so sessions are often in the car. We've had residents who loved the chickens, so guess where those sessions took place? If they love walking, we have walking sessions. If they love art, we do creative activities like beading or drawing while we talk. Sessions can take place while we cook a meal together or garden. Doing sessions in this way is disarming, because it takes the pressure off.

Our milieu counselors are the frontline people who take care of poison ivy, help the girls when they get their periods, talk with them about how to dress properly, and are there for them when they are challenged by the day. We have milieu counselors who are exceptionally kind and caring, who teach the girls how to respect their bodies and how to present themselves. For many of our kids these aren't the battles their parents chose to fight with them.

We focus on providing support to encourage independence, like doing meal prep and making dinner easier for the cooks. A lot of our kids were never shown how to do household chores or were never held into doing them. At Wellspring, the expectation is that each resident contributes to the community. They clean their rooms and make their beds daily. There is a checklist of chores they're accountable for, like rinsing plates after meals, sweeping the floor, cleaning off the tablecloth, putting away food. Parents are surprised and awed by what they do, and their pride in doing it.

There's a constant interplay between staff and residents around daily activities, and a reciprocity has developed between them. For example, we do all of our own shopping, with feedback from the kids about what they like or don't like. When we return from shopping, the kids stop whatever they're doing and help unload the car. Relatedness in these body-experiential ways opens kids' bodies to healing.

Girls who come to Wellspring have often become defined by their symptoms. Many of these symptoms developed as "secondary gains" from the effects of trauma, guilt and shame – such as when a child gets her parents to drop expectations because she's "too sick." But when kids are able to meet their needs directly in response to clear expectations and caring support – which is what we provide through the Shiloah program milieu – symptoms often decrease, and we begin to see who they really are.

ADULT WOMEN'S RESIDENTIAL TREATMENT PROGRAM–ANGELUS HOUSE

Our Adult Residential Treatment Program – located at a separate campus known as Angelus House – serves young adult and adult women age 18 and over. This program serves a wide range of psychiatric and psychological diagnoses including personality, eating, anxiety, post-traumatic, and mood disorders, as well as those who are dually diagnosed with substance abuse in partial remission. Our therapeutic approach is based on the belief that beneath each person's sadness, anger, pain and stress lies an injured self that lacks the foundation of trust necessary for building healthy relationships. Our relational treatment model addresses injuries with both nurturance and structure to reactivate each person's ability to grow in a meaningful way.

Although Angelus serves an older population than our other residential programs, we put a strong focus on parenting here as well. The therapists that lead the program are present and accessible in the house throughout the day. Residents may not be used to "parents" being underfoot in this way, and the clinical structure is different than what they may have encountered at other facilities, but when the relationships are formed, we find that they relax into the milieu, and feel safe.

At Angelus we teach acceptance and self-acceptance, and how to become a functional part of a family and a community. We focus on skill sets including interpersonal effectiveness, emotional regulation, distress tolerance, and mindfulness. But these are not presented in a formalized way so that you trip over them; they're embedded into the daily life of the house. These skills are fundamentally about how to be a healthy human being; how to handle frustration by putting energy into something positive. When these skills are coupled with participation in emotional expressive groups, residents learn how to hold tension and then release their emotions – how to experience, name and express their feelings, especially their anger. At the same time, we provide mindfulness training through yoga, daily meditation, and daily contemplative walks, where everyone is silent, using their senses, being present to immediate experience and not judging.

The milieu teaches values and how to take care of yourself as a way of loving yourself. Simple things like doing daily chores and activities of daily living build healthy ways of living, often replacing chaotic ways. The staff act as role models in this, doing it together with them; this kind of "structuring parent" intervention counteracts the enabling kind of parenting that many of them have experienced before.

While we offer traditional psychotherapy one-to-one in the office, we also do individual therapy in the milieu. We find that providing therapy in the context of everyday life can open greater mutual vulnerability, and more body and heart. In this way, the milieu at Angelus re-translates the basic Wellspring model to respond to the specific residents who come here. The high-nurture and high-structure core remains, and the relational approach is basically the same as in the other programs, but there are changes in texture.

Family therapy is provided according to each resident's need, and while it may be less frequent than in the Adolescent Program, it is an important and potent element of the program. Relationships between residents and parents may be strained, enmeshed or conflicted. We tell residents: "This is for you and about you in terms of what you need from your parents and what they need from you. But know that we will support you and protect you no matter what." And our work in expressive groups helps to free up these relationships.

By bringing these elements together, Angelus House offers a comprehensive treatment program that supports individuals in an intensive treatment process that works to restore themselves and their relationships.

ARCH BRIDGE SCHOOL

Wellspring's Arch Bridge School, founded in 1997 and located on Wellspring's main campus, initially grew out of the need to provide formal education to school-age residents in Wellspring's programs. In the summer of 1990, after serving young adults for the previous thirteen years, Wellspring suddenly found itself with five adolescent clients for whom they would have to provide schooling.

While the school's early days were challenging, over time we have developed a therapeutic education program that embraces the values of Wellspring within the structure of a school program. We seek to nurture, heal, and educate the student whose emotions and/or behavior interfere with the ability to function successfully in school, or in life in general. The Arch Bridge School at Wellspring is now considered by many to be one of the best of its kind in the state and surrounding area.

What began as a two-hour tutorial program at a dining room table eventually became a full school day with several classrooms once we applied to become a Connecticut State Approved Private Special Education Program. Up until that time, school existed to provide an education to the students in residential treatment. Once we were approved by the State, we began taking in day school students who were sent to us by local school districts that were unable to provide an appropriate program for an individual student. We actually thought these kids might be easier to work with since they apparently weren't in need of residential treatment. We soon found out that we'd work all day to help the student make positive changes, only for him or her to return the next morning back at square one. We realized at that point that we needed to intensify the therapeutic component of the program, bridge to outside providers and parents, and to require the involvement of parents through regular Parent Support Groups.

Along with the approval came the requirement that we hire Special Education certified teachers to teach all subject areas. What we were doing instead, and what we fought hard to keep, was hiring subject area certified teachers who could teach on the same level as any area high school teacher and who understood how to teach to the specific needs of the individual. We then trained them to work effectively with students who had mental, emotional, and/or behavioral problems by using the relational model used in Wellspring. It was a system that worked well for both the students that we had in residential treatment, as well as those sent to us by local school districts. Many of the kids, residents in particular, were high functioning students struggling with serious emotional issues. Putting one of these kids in a generic math or science class, as was done in most other treatment facilities at the time, rather than offering them Algebra II, Pre-Calculus, or Chemistry, was not an option. Our goal was to return the student to their home and school district capable of functioning in the classes that their academic level required. In the case of New York State students, this also meant being able to pass the demanding state Regents Exams, which they did. Being able to do this was an important part of their healing.

Our approach with all of the students is to provide a nurturing structure with clear expectations. They come to us defined by their symptoms and labeled by their disability or diagnosis. They challenge us to reject them as others have. We work to let them know that we are on their side in their struggle. We do this by taking every opportunity to show them that we see the essential goodness in them that lies hidden beneath the dysfunctional behavior that got them to us. We try to help them realize that their oppositional, defiant behaviors may once have served them in some way but that it no longer does. We work to help them discover who they really are and to realize they have better, more positive, more effective options for solving their problems.

For our program to work, we need the commitment of both the student and the parents. We have biweekly contact with parents through emails from teachers, phone calls, conferences, or grade reports. In addition, parents are required to participate in Parent Support groups. The school staff keeps in close communication with the residential staff through daily reports received by school staff each morning, attendance in residential groups, and therapeutic staff's attendance in school staff meetings. The Director of Education communicates with school districts through a variety of mechanisms, which is essential to ensure a coordinated approach to specific issues which may arise and to create a workable transition plan for students returning to district or attending a step-down program.

Arch Bridge School follows the Common Core curricula of Connecticut and New York State. We augment learning through land, animal, and adventure programs and through field trips, plays and presentations, community activities, and various vocationally oriented activities, some of which include the use of the greenhouse or kitchen. All are geared to increase each child's sense of capability, love of learning, and success as a student.

Since our goal is always to return a youngster to his or her home and/or school district as soon as they are ready, we have a higher rate of discharge than does a typical private school. This necessitates finding ways to maintain our census. This need is one of the reasons that led us to consider the feasibility of having our school accredited by the New England Association of Schools and Colleges (NEASC). This has enabled us to award our own diplomas and be listed as a fully accredited private school.

The School is approved as a Private Special Education Program and as an Independent Private School by the State of Connecticut. It is approved by New York State Education Department as a 12 Month Out-of-State Residential Program, by New Jersey as an Out-of-State Private School for Students with Disabilities, by Massachusetts as a special education placement for Massachusetts students, by The Joint Commission (TJC) as a Therapeutic School, and is fully accredited by NEASC. We are members of the Litchfield County Directors Association (LCDA) and the Connecticut Association of Private Special Education Facilities (CAPSEF).

The School has been fortunate to have staff throughout its history that are intelligent, creative, and dedicated to helping students become successful in school and in life. The School has developed into the outstanding program that it is because of the many people in all positions who have worked in the program over the years, as well as all those in the general Wellspring community.

This work has borne fruit, as evidenced by the high regard in which the School is held. During our last NEASC survey, the team evaluation stated:

"Educationally and emotionally, the Arch Bridge School is on the leading edge in many of their philosophies and designs. Culturally, Arch Bridge's family atmosphere and unyielding commitment to excellence would be the envy of most schools."

"One of the most outstanding resources of the Arch Bridge School is their staff. They are exceptionally well-trained and deeply passionate about helping and teaching this population... The Arch Bridge School staff experience their mission as transforming, and in many cases, saving lives. This was confirmed time and again by staff at all levels, parents, and the students themselves."

CHAPTER 6

COLLABORATIVE CONVERGENCE: THERAPEUTIC MODES IN WELLSPRING'S INTEGRATED HOLISTIC APPROACH

If a person is awakened into conscious relationship with the matter of creation, then the process of work with the concrete realities of plant, animal, and human bodies becomes healing.

As discussed in Chapter 4, Wellspring's residential treatment programs are comprehensive by intent and design. Through treatment that is multi-modal and holistic in character, we strive to address the body, mind, heart and spirit of each person – combining psychodynamic, cognitive-behavioral, interpersonal interactive, body-experiential, emotional-expressive, and creative-expressive therapies. *Collaborative convergence* of these different therapeutic modalities creates depth and intensity. We implement this convergence through a treatment plan that integrates these modalities in a way that is tailored to the needs of each resident. The development and adaptive implementation of this treatment plan requires intensive communication and coordination across our teams.

In Chapter 5, we explored each of Wellspring's different programs – with a focus on the therapeutic milieu of each. We now turn to the various modalities of treatment that Wellspring incorporates into our integrated therapeutic approach. The backbone of this program is individual and family therapy, supported by outstanding psychiatric and nursing care. But a big part of what makes Wellspring's integrated approach unique is the integration of other therapeutic modes – many of which we have pioneered or substantially adapted to fit our person-centered relational philosophy. These include Work, Animal, Gardening, and Adventure Programs, as well as Expressive Therapy, Art Therapy and Sandtray. The sections that follow – which are adapted from stand-alone essays by, and interviews with, key Wellspring staff in each of these areas – elucidate these modes as we practice them at Wellspring today.

THE CLINICAL "BACKBONE": INDIVIDUAL AND FAMILY THERAPY AND THE MEDICAL DIMENSION OF CARE

Treatment at Wellspring is centered by individual and family therapy. As illustrated in the preceding chapter, milieu therapy in the school and residence supports this work through particular attention to peer and staff relationships. Interactive group therapies concentrate on developing self-assertion, caring feedback, caring confrontation and conflict resolution, and these skills in turn funnel back into the family therapy and parent support and multi-family groups to address issues in family relationships.

In support of this therapeutic work, Wellspring strives to provide the highest level of psychiatric and nursing services to be found in long-term residential treatment and private therapeutic education. Wellspring's founders' training and experience as psychotherapists lay outside of the medical establishment and they sought to create a relational approach to treatment as an alternative to the medical model of care, and to provide this in a homelike environment with milieu therapy at its core. But Wellspring has prided itself on providing quality psychiatry and nursing care. Our model of care guides the use of psychotropic medications, which focuses on supporting the physical, mental and emotional stability each resident needs to participate in Wellspring's different modes of therapy. We work to enable, rather than to suppress, the ability to engage in manual work, recreation, and interpersonal relationship. We provide a safe, nurturing, and well-monitored approach, where medications can be introduced, changed, or discontinued over time.

EXPRESSIVE THERAPY

From the beginning, a central element of Wellspring's integrated therapeutic approach has been Expressive Therapy. Introduced by Phyllis Beauvais, expressive work is a process of body-oriented psychotherapy facilitated through the exploration, expression, and integration of blocked or suppressed feelings utilizing meditative body and expressive techniques (e.g., Psychyodrama, Gestalt, Hakomi, breath work, voice work, play, etc.). It is designed to provide corrective emotional experiences in relationship to self and others through expression, acceptance, validation, and empathy, and can be especially helpful for healing early trauma and attachment injuries.

To support authentic emotional expression, an ambience of safety is essential . In Wellspring's expressive group, a culture of empathy is established, modeled by therapists and willingly followed by all members. The group becomes a sanctuary, an emotionally validating environment where clients learn to build trust. Starting with simple exercises, each client is able to explore her feelings, moving at her own pace through blocks and defenses to deeper levels of emotional expression and release. As she experiences the positive effects of emotional openness and vulnerability in the context of supportive relationships, she becomes more accepting of herself and of her peers. These positive experiences of emotional honesty and depth with peers also support the work of reconnecting with parents and can be further integrated through family therapy.

The ultimate goal of expressive work is insight, emotional integration, self-empowerment, and self-regulation. Expressive work develops internal awareness and connection to the way feelings and emotions manifest in the body, as well as how they can be expressed and regulated consciously and appropriately in the individual's life and relationships. The client learns to be curious about her internal processes and how her needs and feelings motivate behavior. She learns to "be" in her body, to access emotions first as body sensations and then to give vocal expression to her feelings. As she begins to know the "map" of her emotional body by the exploration and practice of expression, she discovers places of rage, pain, and grief, and learns to experience them with consciousness and compassion. Because it is the "truth" of the body and the heart that is experienced in this process, the individual gradually comes to taste the difference between authentic feelings and the substitute symptomatic reactions and externalized acting out that may have dominated her life. She begins to like this taste of truth and is no longer satisfied with pathological substitutes.

WORK PROGRAM

Another modality that is both central and unique to Wellspring's approach is our work program. The use of manual work as a medium for therapeutic healing has deep historical roots. In 1870 the Quaker Friends Hospital used greenhouses and acres of its natural landscape as integral parts of treatment for the mentally ill. At the turn of the century, Dr. Frederick Peterson, a neurologist and head of the New York State Board of Lunacy, did the same with a state asylum. Both the Quakers and Dr. Peterson believed involvement with nature through manual work would be healing.

Although therapeutic work programs have mostly vanished from behavioral health care, manual work in nature remains inherently therapeutic, as many of us know from personal experience. Based on 40+ years of experience with Wellspring's residential treatment programs for adolescents and young adults, we firmly believe that work, therapeutic in its own right, has more importance than ever for behavioral health care – especially for young people. Wellspring's deep, positive experience with work therapy is founded on several fundamental principles.

First, the healing power of manual work is intrinsically tied to involvement with nature – to the physical matter of creation – wood, grass, rocks, soil, plants, animals. In his book, *The Last Child in the Woods,* Richard Louv coined the phrase *nature-deficit disorder*, a non-medical term he uses to describe the unhealthy effects on children of increasing disconnection from nature. Louv cites research showing that teens and tweens spend an average of 7.5 hours per day before screens and 90% of their time indoors. Attention, concentration and cognition are being negatively affected in both direct and subtle ways, which are accompanied by measurable increases in stress, anxiety and depression. These effects are clinically evident in the increasing number of children diagnosed with ADHD. Childhood obesity, a national concern, is directly related to *nature deficit disorder* through inactivity. As children stay indoors, fixated on a cell phone, TV, computer or video games, they suffer accordingly.

On the other hand, research also indicates that direct involvement with nature reduces stress, alleviates depression, and provides an effective alternative to medications used to counteract ADHD. While research about these positive and negative effects is mostly correlational in support of Louv's argument, for the sake of our children, we need to take his research seriously and find corrective ways to respond. From a therapeutic perspective, manual work on the land is well-suited to this purpose.

Children learn about the world firsthand through their senses – touching, tasting, smelling, seeing and hearing. In this respect, withdrawal from the natural to the virtual world causes the sensory world to shrink. The plethora of electronic devices may expand access to information, but sensory experience becomes restricted to the flat screen and keyboard. Social networking presents itself as a tool for expanding relational contact, and it would seem to do that; but the actual experience of participants can be more of isolation than face-to-face contact and exchange. In the documentary film, *Play Again,* one boy says, "I'm in my own little world where I can control what's happening." That's not the same as engagement in the interplay, exchange and tension of relationship. At Wellspring, work programs on the land are combined with adventure program, gardening and animal care – discussed in the sections below – in an effort to restore a healthy balance between exposure to virtual and natural reality.

At Wellspring, we view manual work as a medium to build personal character and interpersonal connection. In this concerted effort, a therapeutic work program confronts three major obstacles, each of which presents both a challenge and a therapeutic opportunity: *Body, Effort* and *Authority*.

Manual work is a body-relational medium. You have to *be* in your body to do it. Manual work compels body presence because of its direct involvement with matter – with the soil, plant, animal and human levels of creation. Being present to a task *in body* requires being in the here-and-now – a piece of work in itself. As Fritz Perls, the originator of Gestalt Therapy used to say, "Get out of your head and come to your senses." Manual work challenges head trips and ways of escape through distraction, ways of disconnection typical of many disorders – *nature-deficit disorder* most of all. Manual work also presses the body to be lived as an instrument – not viewed as an object – and body image concerns must give way to experience of the functional body, true even for anorectics who can misuse it for over-exercise.

A second obstacle to work is *effort*. Manual work takes physical exertion and, consequently, draws upon all the qualities of personality and character that effort can engender – patience, persistence, endurance, focused aggression, care and attention, will and will power – the list is endless. These are all ego strengths, and as such they are the very stuff of personal growth and character building at the core of treatment. Surely the development of a strength comes from its exercise, and manual work requires the ability to *do hard things*, to expend oneself energetically and go beyond one's sense of limitation. This builds self-confidence while a sense of accomplishment builds self-esteem.

A third obstacle to manual work is *authority*: Who or what am I working for or under, as the case may be? Authority comes from the Latin *auctor*, which means *to author, to originate, to bring forth and create*. At Wellspring, the authority of a staff member is based on her ability to author the resident into personal growth and healing through the medium of work. The authority of the resident, on the other hand, comes from learning to exercise authority over herself, by directing her energy into the work task, and by learning how to take charge of it with personal empowerment.

For a work program to become a therapy in its own right, the work also must relate to the individual's treatment process as an integral part of treatment planning. This involves the *subjective* dimension of work, where the work experience can be focused on issues specific to the individual – where work becomes a way of *working on oneself*. To the degree that a work program does this, along with its more general goals, the legal problem of exploitation is resolved. It can also respond to challenging questions from residents such as, "Why should I work? What does this have to do with me? I'll never have to muck stalls or mess with animals, dig a ditch, plant flowers, whatever. Wellspring should be paying me to work." This is where a therapeutic work program can be developed into an art.

The first requirement for a work therapist is to know the work task intimately from personal experience. This knowledge is both external and internal, both physical and psychological. By experiencing and reflecting on each task – weeding, raking, digging, lifting, shoveling manure – the work therapist comes to understand the qualities of personality, the particular ego strengths each task requires of the worker. These strengths are revealed by the *interior* demands a task makes through its physical demands. Tasks can then be chosen to address relevant issues, whether to utilize and build upon an existing strength, or to address a weakness in need of development. The work therapist can then articulate why she has assigned a particular task and invite the person to take on the *inner work* of the task for self-development. The trite generality – "this work will be good for you" – becomes redefined into a specific opportunity for growth and healing.

To fit the task to the person in terms of treatment issues and objectives, the work therapist has to know each individual both clinically and as a worker. Work histories intertwine with clinical and relational histories that affect a resident's attitude toward manual work. Parenting is important in this regard, especially in terms of expectations about work and relationship to authority. In assessing this dimension, the work therapist becomes aware of responses and reaction patterns that emerge in work that may be unconscious to the resident. They can also affect how the individual relates to different kinds of work and different kinds of matter, like soil, leaves, rocks, wood and manure, their smells and textures. As these response patterns emerge in various tasks and contexts, they can be addressed, reframed, re-decided and even changed in the course of treatment. A girl who arrived from New York City saying, "I don't do cows," fell in love with a young calf and its care and ended up baking a cake and feeding it joyfully to her calf when she was discharged!

Assessment of the individual as a worker – how she actually functions in work – is best obtained through close observation with different kinds of work. As the work therapist reads *the body of the worker* in response to different tasks, strengths and weaknesses are revealed through the non-verbal language of energy, movement, breathing, posture, alertness and alacrity. This body language will then guide her interventions.

Work program is also a medium for developing relational skills with peers, as well as with persons in authority. Work projects can be structured around interdependence, like stacking firewood in a chain where each log is handed from one person to another, drawing upon attunement. Where this is lacking, friction develops that needs to be worked out on site or in group therapy. On the other hand, side-by-side cooperation in working for a common good leads to shared satisfaction and mutual affirmation. Both the frictional and cooperative experiences provide raw material for learning self-assertion, affirmation, caring feedback, "staying in the tension," and conflict resolution – necessary skills for any relationship.

As a dimension of a therapeutic work program, work as *a visible statement of values in action* is the medium for developing a positive work ethic. The work therapist can help this process by modeling and encouragement, but the natural world provides its own feedback about the quality of the work. A structure stands or falls, animals are contented or disgruntled, flowers bloom or die, the meal is edible and enjoyable – or not. Continuity of context in which this flow of feedback can happen is important for the development of a work ethic to occur.

At Wellspring, we strive to integrate all these elements in our program of work therapy: involvement with nature, character building, and focused interventions for the treatment of core issues. This program is integrated, in turn, within our overall framework of a multi-modal, process-oriented, relational treatment.

ANIMAL PROGRAM

Wellspring has been home to farm animals from its earliest days, when Richard and Phyllis Beauvais brought goats with them to the main campus on Arch Bridge Road. From the start, we incorporated care of animals into Wellspring's work program. As more effort and resources were dedicated to the needed expansion of educational and outpatient services, the land-based programs were, for a time, marginalized. In 2004, Wellspring's Board of Directors made a strategic decision to reinvigorate our connection with animals and the land. One important result of this direction was the reestablishment of a full-fledged Animal Program, available to all of our programs.

The content of the Animal Program at Wellspring can be designated professionally as "Animal Assisted Activities. Our assistants in this work are farm animals – sheep, goats, chickens, barn cats, and an occasional rabbit.

Wellspring approaches the treatment of severe emotional disorders through the primary medium of relationship. This approach is especially relevant for the treatment of attachment difficulties – addressing early trauma and its effects on the emotional and relational attachment of the child to the parents – where issues of care, trust, dependability, safety and closeness are of central concern. Relationship with animals is valuable in this approach, particularly in the treatment of children, where non-verbal experience is more effective than verbal-cognitive methods alone. These relationships also provide opportunities for positive, non-threatening, and comforting touch.

At Wellspring, we place tremendous importance on contact with and care for animals. Animal care requires a daily commitment to the welfare of another being. But most importantly, animals, by their nature, offer direct exposure to an instinctual level of being, allowing individuals to reconnect to their own instinctive and unconscious drives. In comparison to the complexity of human-to-human relationships, there is a simple and pure quality to relationship with an animal. An animal's "integrity," if you will, lies in its "wholeness" and "trueness" to itself. An animal is wholly itself at all times; there are no projections, no personae, no relational games. If one chooses to relate to an animal, one must take the animal as it is, accepting its actions at face value.

For a child or an adolescent who has learned to distrust adults, the safety in relating to an animal is palpable. The animal is real, vital, capable of interacting with a human, but it is not "out to get you" – there is no malice, no hidden agenda. The animal will learn to trust you, if you are trustworthy. It will depend on you for food, if you feed it. And it will learn to receive and enjoy affection from you, if you are gentle and respond to its needs. Taking care of an animal provides a safe and meaningful way to begin to develop a relationship with that animal. And that relationship, in turn, is a safe place to begin to learn to care, to be affectionate, to explore assertiveness, to feel angry without lashing out, to feel free to be oneself.

Animals offer a remarkably "clean" medium for person-to-person relationship as well. They provide a reason to relate to another person, a creative "third" element for two people to focus on, which can aid in bridging otherwise difficult gaps. In the residential setting, this is often very helpful, particularly at the beginning of a resident's stay. Contact with an animal can melt the hard exterior that a child, adolescent or young adult often presents, as he or she responds out of attraction, repulsion or fascination. An animal provides a compelling subject that the resident can focus on, and the conversation with the counselor can then be a "safe" one about the animal rather than the resident. Often people are distracted and comforted by the presence of an animal, causing them to be more open than perhaps otherwise. Moreover, an animal's trust in the adult staff person, and its willingness to accept nurturing and affection, "proves" in some way that the adult is a trustworthy and safe person for the resident.

As discussed in the section on Work Program above, greater contact with nature provides tremendous benefits for young residents, helping them to de-stress and bolstering their resiliency. Work with an animal gets one out of one's busy mind and into one's body. It offers a break from all the talk and becomes a rich source of meaningful therapeutic metaphors. For young adult residents, it allows them to address treatment goals in a real-life situation, as they grapple with their responses in completing a task, while interacting with peers and staff.

Our first priority is to take care of the animals' physical needs – food, water, a clean stall, grooming. The feeding and caring for these "others" – these animals – offers a context for learning about feeding and caring for one's own body. As a resident assumes responsibility for an animal's care, she becomes attentive to its bodily needs. Residents seem to identify with their charges, and often will speak on behalf of any perceived needs of the animals. The desire to improve the feed or the environment of the animal may eventually influence the resident, consciously or unconsciously, to discover the same desire for herself. The love that develops for the animal's body evokes a desire to provide for the animal's comfort. This, in turn, can move the resident to love and care for her own body – or at least it becomes a place to begin the conversation.

After the animals have been taken care of physically, there is opportunity for interactions and projects. This often depends on group size, interests, the weather, and the animals' needs. This could involve just "being with" the animals, holding them, playing with them, building a relationship. Or it could involve building something to improve their environment.

The core values we foster through working with animals include *empathy*, *emotional awareness* and *attunement*, *relationship*, *responsibility* and *humane education*. To teach these values, we use a relational triad involving the client, the animal, and the handler. The handler must rely on her relationship with the client and her familiarity with the animal to bring them together. Trust has to be built in both, and trust takes time.

With *empathy*, the question is – are you able to look outside of yourself? Can you see or imagine how another feels? Crises, for example, can be opportunities for learning empathy. When Micasa, one of our sheep, broke her leg and spent over a month recovering in a stall, the kids responded. They were able to baby her and also get closer to her during that time. The same thing happened with an older ewe, who went blind towards the end of her life. The kids would gather grass for her to eat and brought her treats and often asked how she was doing.

***Emotional awareness* and *attunement* involve knowing what you are feeling, for the animals will pick this up and respond/react to it. But can you also read how the animal is feeling? Can you comfort the animal, or allow yourself to be comforted?** For younger children, where non-verbal experience is usually more effective than talk, relationship with an animal can provide key steps early in their treatment. A relationship also provides opportunities for positive, non-threatening, and comforting touch – brushing a goat, petting a cat, holding and stroking a chicken.

As for *relationship*, can you engage or be with another? Can you cooperate with another? Contact with animals and their care has great value for our young people, because of the rich opportunities to learn about relationship. Taking care of an animal offers a safe and meaningful way to develop a relationship, and that relationship, in turn, is a safe place to begin to care, to be affectionate, to explore assertiveness, and to feel empathy for another.

In terms of *responsibility*, it can be hard to care for another, because sometimes it rains or snows. It takes discipline and constancy, because sometimes you might not want to go down to the barn and feed the animals. But **because these animals are dependent on us, we have to respond to their needs, not just our own. Responsibility is rooted in our ability to respond.**

With *humane education*, the link between violence toward animals and violence toward persons must always be kept in mind. Because some of our children have this propensity, we must be vigilant and cautious. For if we allow animal cruelty to occur, we have allowed the child to re-injure herself. Therefore, the values we teach and try to instill through the care of animals have longer-term social impact. The difference in working with animals, in contrast to working with wood, creating a song, or painting a canvas, is that these are living, sentient beings. At all times we need to be aware of this, because animals have rights and freedoms that we are morally obligated to provide for when we take on their care. Everything else we do depends on this, for if the structures of care are not upheld, the capacity for nurture will suffer.

In all of this, we take as fundamental that we are working *with* animals in partnership – not *using* animals for treatment and education. Because this is a partnership, we must include the animals by looking at things from their perspective, their life. To the degree we do so, we can enter their lives, and wonderful things can happen. It's actually very simple. Rather than "I want to hold a chick," does the chick want to be held? And how can we do this in a way that's pleasant for her? It means advocating for the animals while working with our residents. We hold structure for their interaction and relationship.

When we create a space in which structure and nurture are balanced – where trust can be established between the resident and the animal – a relationship can form that opens the resident to healing in remarkable ways.

GARDEN PROGRAMS

Another form of work or land-based therapy we provide at Wellspring is therapeutic gardening programs – working through the medium of the beautiful cottage gardens and vegetable gardens that surround our campuses. Gardening provides a medium to implement the values of work therapy described above – including a focus on relation to nature and development of character and relationship.

At Wellspring, we see the garden as *a place of mystery*, a place of spirit, where one can connect with a creative force and see what comes from it. From above and below there is an energy in the sun and the earth that holds the plant upright, feeding its roots and branches. Working with adolescents, just like with a garden, you never know quite where the seed will grow. The garden is constantly creating itself in one way or another. Gardening has been described as "the slowest of the performing arts," with its flowering progression through the season. There's an innocence in plants, and it's amazing to see how the garden can bring out the child in a person. Work in the garden also reveals something about who the person is underneath their surface behavior.

The garden should be a zone of safety, a non-judgmental place. Plants have needs and people have needs, and a person comes into a "child" state in the garden only by feeling safe. A plant will let you know what it needs if you observe it, and so will a child. Quietness and attunement are important in working with an individual side by side. One resident said, insightfully, that the garden is "a place to be seen" – seen through the work of being a weeder, a pruner, a trimmer, or a digger of holes for planting. The task becomes a way of revealing the person and not just a chore.

The garden is rich in analogy, which is the language of metaphor and simile. Analogies form a bridge between the internal and the external, where the two can meet peacefully. A garden is multi-layered with its surface of chores, dirt, someone else's structure, cold, heat, someone else's ideas. People often can't see the work going on beneath their work. But in a garden, nature itself holds a depth of process through the seasons that can best be grasped through analogy in mirroring process back to them.

Because we are part of nature, our lives reflect her cycles, and this is especially true with healing. When someone is in intensive treatment, her growth may not be evident, for her behaviors at times may seem more problematic than ever. Winter in New England is a time of important growth – we just can't see it. This is a time when a plant gets stronger, strengthening its roots and preparing for spring. Then in the spring, suddenly the garden is full of vigorous new life and we are all surprised, pleased and relieved, for winter gets very old up here. But without winter, a New England spring would not be so breathtaking. Without the dying of leaves in fall, there would be no spring. Without the sun and rain of summer, there would be no garden. The analogies are endless and may often seem clichéd, but they are bearable because they are deep and true. In therapeutic gardening, we trust that *being* communicates. Process is always cyclical, seasonal – whether that happens in a day or in a year – and our residents come to understand that.

Similarly, pruning, like cutting back on distractions or bad habits, can strengthen a plant or tree just as it can a person. Weeds can be likened to defenses – or "misplaced" plants. Weeding and pruning are about editing, letting go, bringing order to something disordered. Planting bulbs, which we do in the fall, draws something different out of us. These activities are about beginnings and hope and keeping things underground where they can be safe to grow silently. The child also needs a place to work safely, because at first she's too vulnerable for direct exposure. The garden is a place to see and understand that and have it mirrored back from nature.

At Wellspring, gardening is an important part of our effort to restore a relationship with nature. Residents are often uncomfortable in their bodies and tend to relate to soil as dirt, not as part of the earth from which things grow. They can also be "entitled" and hate work and see physical labor as second class. They're often resistant saying, "Why do I have to do this?" But the resistance gradually becomes quieter, and the attitude "I am not doing this ever" subsides. We work to help them make that passage from gardening as a "chore" to a growth process linking them to their own growth. This occurs only gradually and sometimes not at all, but when it does there's an awakening.

"Mother Nature" is both structure and nurture side by side. The land and the garden offer infinite opportunities for nurture, but nurture can occur only if the structures are clear and in place. For example, we had a resident whose sister had died in a car accident and she had done extraordinary work in art therapy grieving her sister and was beginning to bring this to groups. The garden gave her a place to just "be" while working side by side with a mothering person. In this case, the garden provided the structure that could hold whatever she needed to say, because weeding was not the goal, but only the occasion.

There are times when the garden has to do with learning about structure, the demands of work, and the demands of working with others, and one of our goals is to teach residents how to work. There is work as work and work as fun. A few times a year, we hold community workdays – creating a new garden space behind the Chapel Barn or raking leaves, or cleaning up neglected spaces, or planting bulbs. For some of us that work is fun. Each of us, resident or staff, is participating to the fullest of our ability. Whether it's the heavy work of digging up roots, or gently finding a place to put one more bulb, we are working together, improving the land. These are experiences that are difficult to describe – but ones that we at Wellspring see as rich in meaning and deeply valuable.

ADVENTURE PROGRAM

The other principal land-based therapy we offer at Wellspring is Adventure Program – which focuses on engaging residents in fun physical activities to help them develop a sense of self. Many of our residents have never really learned how to play, how to be a child again, and how to enjoy the people around them. They tend to be very entrenched in their problems and how bad *they* feel, which can make them oblivious to the lives of others. We work to overcome that by getting them engaged in physical activity.

We have a ropes course at the main campus, but we also go off grounds to facilities with other challenges including ziplines or high ropes courses. The challenge for some may be just to put a harness on or go over to the mini-course, which is only five feet off the ground and not so scary. Everything in the program is "challenge by choice." Individuals need permission to say "No," in order to come to their "Yes." One of the things they particularly love is going to the "mystery room." The mystery room involves six of them at a time working together to solve a mystery. We also hike a lot in White Memorial, Steep Rock, and local nature preserves where our runners can get to run. We also have many different group games and trust skills activities that challenge them to work together.

The Program also plays an essential role in helping residents to develop a sense of community. Often when the community is going through a difficult time, we'll go out on the ropes course where the girls have to cooperate and work together to solve problems. In order to get over "the wall" as a group, for example, they have to use both the strengths and weaknesses in the group to be able to do that. They have to pull together, otherwise it just won't happen. As a result, they always come back kinder – with greater empathy for one another.

In all of the above, the first and most important thing is to get kids moving, get them out of their heads and into their bodies. When their bodies get free, their minds get free.

ART THERAPY

Art therapy uses artistic expression to allow residents to access and heal psychological wounds. Through the use of creative techniques such as drawing, painting, coloring, collage, and clay work, art speaks what can't be said in words and what may not even be conscious. It can help to awaken memories and tell stories that may reveal emotional obstacles, messages, or beliefs hidden in the unconscious mind. Through the creative externalization of inner processes, the resident is able to discover and choose new pathways which more authentically reflect her growing sense of self.

At Wellspring, our art therapists work to help residents explore, express, and gradually understand themselves, believing that the act of creating is healing in itself. We encourage each resident to honor and experience her own creativity (art therapy does not require artistic talent in the conventional sense). Experienced in an atmosphere of safety and acceptance, the exploration of color, texture, and the various media allow an emerging comfort in risking spontaneity of self-expression. Symbolic, visual, and kinesthetic, this modality bypasses the limitations of language and engages mind, heart, and soul. Valuable in and of itself, when used in complement with our other modes of therapy, it supports personal and relational insight and enhances social skills, family awareness, and community involvement.

Art therapy was one of Richard's favorite modalities, and early residents were privileged to experience his facility in combining dreamwork with artistic exploration. Each of the art therapists who has joined us at Wellspring over the past four-plus decades has brought her own unique style and gifts in engaging our residents, while sharing our community values and our love for this work.

SANDTRAY THERAPY

Another creative-expressive therapy currently used at Wellspring is Sandtray, a Jungian method of imaginal therapy that involves metaphoric play. The method did not originate with Jung but with some of his disciples, who first called it "Sandplay". Although similar to Play Therapy in some respects, there are differences. Objects are chosen and placed in a sandtray with the intent to tell a personal story, a spontaneous narrative that connects consciousness with the unconscious. Always fluid and changeable, it expresses whatever emerges in that day or in the moment.

The tray itself is a rectangular box 20 x 30 x 4 inches deep. It forms a universe of its own, small enough for the creator to see the whole and take in both sides at once. Its interior is painted blue, imaging water and the sky, although it may not have that meaning for the person doing it. The sand is finely ground, sensuous to the touch. We use white sand, which can be either wet or dry. The person can make images in the sand, including by using elements such as stones.

The idea is for the person creating the Sandtray to tell a story without interpretation and for all to treat that story as sacred. During the work, some people talk but most do not. The process takes one to two hours, and the creator usually becomes deeply immersed in the work. The experience itself is ineffable. Whatever happens, happens deep within the person. When they come back from it, usually they're shocked that so much time has passed. Although some Sandtrays are filled with anger, it seems the person no longer carries it within them. The story is out in the box, but they're not infused with it. We find that Sandtray is especially valuable for individuals who have difficulty putting their thoughts, feelings and memories into words. For kids with learning difficulties that interfere with verbal articulation, for example, Sandtray helps bridge that gap because it comes from a different center of the brain.

The fact that a Sandtray won't be interpreted is immensely reassuring and is key to the whole process. Anyone who has suffered trauma, whether she is conscious of it or not, is reassured by the freedom to decide whether or not to share a Sandtray. There is no pressure or coercion to disclose. We assure them that the work has already been done and it doesn't matter if anyone else knows the story; we urge them to just live with what they've experienced in the doing of it.

While a Sandtray is always created by a single individual, kids may choose to present their Sandtray to a group, though there's no obligation to do so. This kind of group presentation teaches people more about a person they thought they already knew. Residents who have heard from their peers about this medium often ask if they could do a Sandtray and tell their story. We find that kids have a deep urgency to do this, to be heard. Just having objects outside of oneself to point to, being able to use symbols and images, allows them to speak more freely. Sandtray group is a beautiful way to foster attunement to one another.

Over time, Sandtray therapy can both support and reflect growth and healing. One girl did a Sandtray every week for over a year. Her initial Sandtray was a line in the sand reflecting the "good" side of her brain and the "bad" side; then she filled the box with everything she could think of. Certain figures showed up every time, and the sand slowly became clearer with spaces in between. Mandala forms began to appear gradually at first with disruptions in them. She always represented herself as a different animal or beast, then kinder animals, but never as a person. She knew that others also experienced her that way as an animal. She represented her mother, a woman who had suffered greatly, as a beautiful hand with the sun in the middle of it. In her final Sandtray, she created a tunnel with an animal going in and a person coming out the other end. It was a perfect mandala in circular form with the tunnel forming the center. Her mother was on the other side of the tunnel as a woman now accompanied by an open hand with the sun in it. That was her work – becoming human – embodying herself in her essential goodness, which she had despaired of ever achieving. She had found her way back to herself and to a loving relationship with another person, which is the real work of Wellspring. It was the realization of her own inner treatment plan.

CONCLUSION

The array of therapeutic modes described above provide the building blocks of Wellspring's integrated approach to treatment. But as explained above, the therapeutic art is in integrating these elements in a collaborative convergent model of care – which requires intensive communication and cooperation among staff. When this is done well, it allows for a whole of integrated care that far transcends the sum of the parts – with insights and advances gained in each mode helping to inform and improve the others – all in the service of personal and relational healing.

CHAPTER 7

CENTERING IN THE STILL POINT

The future of Wellspring has never been under our control.

Like any child, or any destiny, we simply meet what unfolds before us, holding fast to our values and intentions to heal.

Dedicated in 1980, Wellspring's Still Point Chapel originally stood behind what is now the administration building at Wellspring's main campus. This simple wood frame structure, once a horse stall, became a chapel with a woodstove, an altar, a crucifix, and a few benches. It provided a sacred space for prayer, meditation and, on occasion, for celebrating Mass. Outwardly, it stood as a visible sign and reference to a greater good, both grounding and calling forth the healing mission of Wellspring.

When the Still Point Chapel became structurally unsafe, it was dismantled and a process of relocation and reconstruction began. This challenge, taken up by the Board of Directors, raised many questions – about placement, the relevance of a Chapel to the foundational philosophy and values, and what form it might take to serve the Wellspring of today and tomorrow. Ultimately, the Board decided to build what is now the Chapel Barn – which unites a chapel, a place of meditation and spiritual centering, with the barn where we house and care for our animals. This was a return to Wellspring's roots and an expression of our fundamental values. As Richard explained:

> "THE TOUCHSTONE OF OUR APPROACH TO TREATMENT IS A BELIEF THAT WITHIN EACH INDIVIDUAL THERE IS A WELLSPRING OF PERSONAL BEING THAT IS UNIQUE, UNREPEATABLE AND IMBUED WITH SPIRIT. CHILDREN FIRST ENTER THIS MYSTERY THROUGH THE DOORWAY OF THE ANIMALS, WHO REVEAL TO US OUR ESSENTIAL INNOCENCE, HOWEVER INJURED, THROUGH THE TRANSPARENT REALITY OF THEIR OWN. THEREFORE, IT IS FITTING THAT A CHAPEL AT WELLSPRING SHOULD BE A BARN – A MANGER OF SIMPLICITY AND SILENCE – A PLACE TO EXPERIENCE EACH LEVEL OF OUR BEING AS PARTICIPANTS IN THE GREATER MYSTERY OF CREATION."

In her book, *Devotion: A Memoir*, Dani Shapiro, a Bethlehem resident, wrote of her experience after visiting the Chapel Barn:

> "I CLIMBED THE WOODEN STEPS TO THE AUSTERE INTERIOR OF THE CHAPEL. IT WAS FREEZING INSIDE, THE WIND WHIPPING THROUGH IT. I FIGURED THEY MUST NOT BE DONE BUILDING IT YET. THE CHAPEL ITSELF WAS EMPTY OF FURNISHING, SAVE FOR A LOW BENCH THAT RAN ROUND THE PERIMETER OF THE ROOM. THE LATE-AFTERNOON SUN CAST ITS LAST LIGHT ACROSS THE FLOORBOARDS. I STOOD IN THE CENTER OF THE CHAPEL AND BREATHED IN DEEPLY. THE AIR STILL SMELLED OF NEW WOOD, BUT THERE WAS SOMETHING ELSE. A SURPRISING SCENT. IT TOOK ME A MOMENT TO REALIZE THAT THE CHAPEL WAS A HAYLOFT.
>
> THEY WERE DONE BUILDING. THE WALLS DIDN'T MEET THE FLOOR. THE WIND WHIPPING THROUGH HAD BEEN INTENTIONAL. THE SMELL OF HAY, OF BARN LIFE. NATURE WOULD ALWAYS BE PRESENT IN THIS SPACE. THE INTERIOR AND EXTERIOR WORLDS SEAMLESS, EXISTING IN CONCERT. I HAD AN IMAGE, THEN, OF MY FATHER'S CASKET AT HIS FUNERAL. THAT SIMPLE, PLAIN PINE BOX. MEANT TO FALL APART IN THE GROUND. DUST TO DUST. I TOOK ANOTHER DEEP BREATH. I WAS A LITTLE CHOKED UP, AND TRIED TO GET A GRIP ON MYSELF... WHAT WAS IT ABOUT THIS PLACE? IT FELT...SACRED. JUST STANDING THERE FELT LIKE A FORM OF PRAYER. PRECISELY BECAUSE OF ITS EMPTINESS, IT VIBRATED WITH ALL OF LIFE."

Wellspring has experienced tremendous growth and change since its humble beginnings in 1977. That growth is like a living tree which must root deeply to provide stability for the branching out of new life. As we continue the unfolding history of Wellspring – and especially as we transition beyond the era in which Wellspring's founders have been present to guide its growth – it is essential that we recall and deepen our understanding of our roots, our foundational values, and the philosophy and Spirit which both ground and guide us. We need to nourish these roots, and in so doing, communicate them to the body of staff that will bring Wellspring's healing work into the future.

For those who have lived its history, nothing is clearer than that Wellspring will live or die in the Spirit. If the spirit of Wellspring fades or becomes diluted, then Wellspring's uniqueness will die with it. Without reference to this spiritual ground, practical expediency can take over and the wellspring we draw from can go dry. The Chapel Barn both marks this reality and underscores Wellspring's continuing mission.

Before the entrance to the Still Point Chapel, placed opposite to the Wellspring Logo, this framed invitation written by Phyllis is hung by the doorway to welcome visitors:

A place for silence, meditation, and prayer

A Sacred Space

You are invited to enter with an attitude of reverence

"Be still and know that I am God"

A place to breathe, center, and "just be"

A place to tap into your inner wellspring

A place to center yourself and your intentions

A place to lift up your joy, sorrow, longing, anger, and fear

A place to remember your hope and your gratitude

A place to ground yourself in The Good Creation

A place to connect with Spirit

A place to listen for "the still small voice" within

We have lived through much change over the past forty-plus years since Wellspring's founding. God willing, there is much more change and growth to come – many chapters yet to be written in the Book of Wellspring. Although our original barn was long ago turned into administrative and clinical offices, and our original Still Point Chapel was dismantled, the Chapel Barn we have now becomes and symbolizes the new, revitalized place where we can center ourselves and remember our founding values and vision.

CREDITS AND ACKNOWLEDGEMENTS

We are beyond grateful to the generous contributions of our friends and colleagues who have infused their gifts into the flow and fabric of Wellspring.

There are many who have helped make a profound impact on the evolution of Wellspring and there will be others in our future. The friends listed below have taken the time to be interviewed for the book, collaborated with us to write sections, and have given overall guidance to this beloved project. A special thank you goes to our son Joel Beauvais for editing the Book of Wellspring.

*Michael Ackerman	Celia Pomerantz
*Cassandra Beauvais	Rev. Francis Prokes, SJ
Joe Braccio	Christina Reddington
Liz Bunovsky	Joyce Rubenstein
Margaret Colliton	Janet Samela-Sorrell
Jeff Culhane	Holly Savage
Kathy Dowling	Ralph Scafariello
David Ferguson	*Susan Scott Schoenbach
Brett Beauvais Fisher	*Dani Shapiro
Ann Light	Deb Talmadge
Joe Mancinone	The Abbey of Regina Laudis
Mike Marques	The Franciscan Sisters of the Eucharist
Tom McDermott	Sara Van Doren
Dan Murray	Ann Watson
Michele Murelli	
Marty Newell	*contributing author

And last but not least, the compassionate oversight of our Board of Directors:

Michael Ackerman	Libby Graham
Babette Basil	Cynthia Hallenbeck-Libby
Joel Beauvais	Bill and Jill Hogan
Michael and Kathy Berkowitz	Tom Jasper
Jim Donaghy	Melodee Morrison
Roger Duncan	Peggy and Jerry Sturman
Rachel Gately	Rev. Robert Tucker

Printed in Poland
by Amazon Fulfillment
Poland Sp. z o.o., Wrocław